A Lancashire Look:

A Lancashire Book

Benita Moore A.L.A.

("A Lancashire Native")

Landy Publishing
1996

ISBN 1-872895-30-1

Landy Publishing have also published:

In Lancashire Language, dialect verse edited by Bob Dobson

Concerning Clogs by Bob Dobson

A Blackburn Miscellany, edited by Bob Dobson

An Accrington Mixture, edited by Bob Dobson

Accrington Observed by Brian Brindle and Bob Dobson

In Fine Fettle (dialect verse) by Peter Thornley and Michael May

Blackburn's West End by Matthew Cole

Blackburn's Shops at the Turn of the Century by Matthew Cole

and publish the quarterly

"Really Lancashire: a magazine for the Red Rose County"

Landy Publishing, 3 Staining Rise, Staining, Blackpool, FY3 0BU
tel/fax: 01253 895678

All books ordered from Landy Publishing are sent post-free to U.K. addresses.

Details of Benita Moore's previous books may be obtained from her at
156 Rising Bridge Road, Haslingden, BB4 5BH
tel: 01706 215914

Layout by Mike Clarke, Accrington, tel: 01254 395848

Printed by Nayler the Printer Ltd, Accrington, tel: 01254 234247/8/9

Contents

The Mobile Library and some of 'my readers'.

INTRODUCTION

Those of you who have read my previous book about my travels with the Ramsbottom Mobile Library: *"A Lancashire Year"*, will know how much I enjoyed the work and especially seeing the lovely little villages and their warm-hearted Lancashire inhabitants. Indeed, it wasn't work, it was a pleasure, and so many people have asked for further tales about the Mobile Library and my 'dear readers', that in 1995-6, using my Nature Diary and Personal Diary, I have written a second volume about the time when I returned to the job for a second period.

Oh, but how lovely it was to trundle around the villages and see once more each changing season bring its own individual beauty. The greening hawthorn and frothing forsythia; the perfume of lilac and roses and the stalwart hills of Lancashire glorious in purple heather and bronzed bracken. How my heart rejoiced as I renewed acquaintances with those warm-hearted, whimsical Lancashire folk, for these were 'my readers', not just people who borrowed books, but people with whom I shared life's joys and sorrows and formed a lasting friendship.

It should be stated that most of the names in the book are fictional and any references to people with a similar name or characteristic are purely co-incidental. There are however, one or two people who were 'my readers' on the Mobile Library so many years ago and are still using the library in 1996. They have very kindly given me permission to use their real names and for this I thank them, as they were delighted to be involved in this second book about my adventures on the Mobile Library.

In 1974, the 'Ramsbottom Regional Library Service' was dispersed due to Local Government Reorganisation, but the Mobile Library still runs from Rawtenstall I'm happy to say. So, dear readers, I hope you enjoy reading about my adventures in Lancashire as much as I've enjoyed writing about them.

BENITA MOORE
September 1996

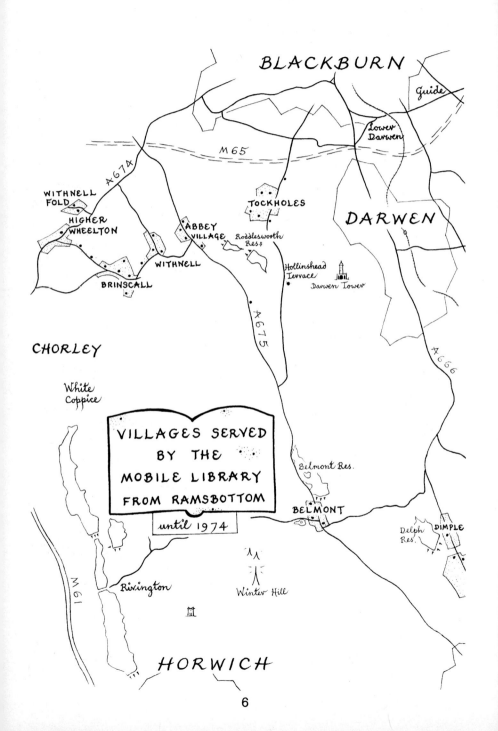

BLACKBURN

Guide

Lower Darwen

M 65

A 674

DARWEN

WITHNELL FOLD

TOCKHOLES

HIGHER WHEELTON

ABBEY VILLAGE

Roddlesworth Ress

WITHNELL

Hollinshead Terrace

BRINSCALL

Darwen Tower

A 675

CHORLEY

A 666

White Coppice

VILLAGES SERVED BY THE MOBILE LIBRARY FROM RAMSBOTTOM

until 1974

Belmont Res.

BELMONT

Delph Res.

DIMPLE

M 61

Rivington

Winter Hill

HORWICH

6

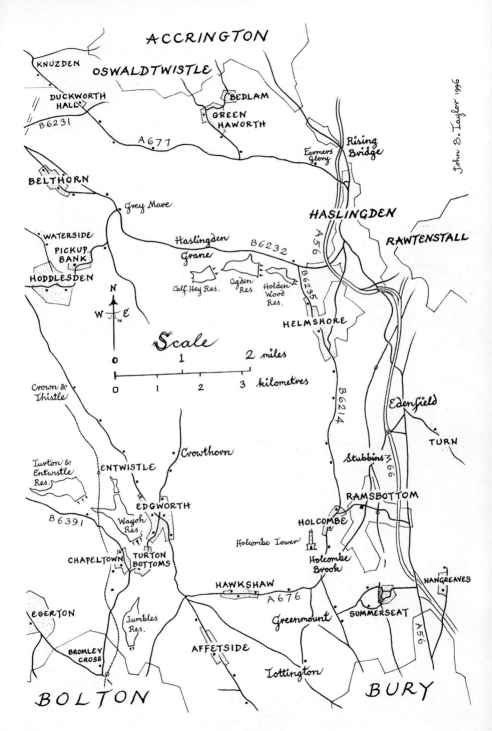

Two Belmont ladies, Mrs. Holden on the right, make their selection from the van's stock.

The author behind the library's counter.

8

A LANCASHIRE NATIVE

It was a warm sunny March morning in the early 1970s. I was washing-up in the kitchen of my new house at Rising Bridge, a semi-rural village between Accrington and Haslingden. And oh, how lovely it was washing-up when I could look out of the window at the same time and see the glory of the hills of Rossendale, the tiny cottages like 'Sherfin Nook', the farms and rural homesteads which faced me in the distance across the main road. Directly opposite our house on the other side of Rising Bridge Road was the defunct Accrington/Manchester railway line on which I used to travel to Ramsbottom before I could drive when I had a job as the Mobile Librarian there. I was hoping to be re-instated in the same job soon.

A thousand tiny coltsfoot flowers on the wasteland opposite turned their sunny faces towards the windows and smiled at me. I smiled back, content in my work and the fact that I could delight in so much of the lovely Lancashire countryside from my own home. Penny and Heidi, my two young daughters, were happily playing on the heathered hillside next to our home. I heard the letterbox rattle and a 'plop' as the day's batch of letters were delivered. Drying my hands, I went to pick them up. My heart missed a beat as I shuffled through the envelopes. Would it be there, the one I was waiting for so ardently? I recognised it – the familiar long brown envelope stamped 'Lancashire County Council'. My fingers trembled as I opened it.

> Dear Mrs. Moore,
> Re your application for the post of Mobile Librarian at the Ramsbottom Divisional Library, we are pleased to inform you...etc, etc, etc.

I gave a huge shout that brought Penny and Heidi running to my side. *"I've got it, I've got it, I'm going back to work on the Mobile Library again."* Penny's blue eyes looking at me so candidly, as if she thought me quite ridiculous, made me calm down a little. *"The job my darlings, my favourite job on the Mobile Library at Ramsbottom. Now that you're both at school, I can have my old job back."* I took their hands and danced round the dining-room, my heart rejoicing as I thought how lovely it would be to see those warm-hearted Lancashire villagers once more. *"Mum! Does that mean we can miss Sunday School when you're at work?"* asked Penny. *"Certainly not! I don't work on Sunday,"* I told them firmly. They ran outside to continue their games and I smiled at their innocent concept of things.

9

Bless their hearts, neither they nor my husband, Gordon, could understand my delight in Mother Nature and her bounties, nor why my foolish romantic heart longed so much for fresh air, space and freedom, plus the joy of socialising with fellow Lancastrians.

I went back to the washing-up, splashing the water and forming bubbles which I blew around the kitchen like a child. In each rainbowed sphere, I saw images of *'my dear readers'* (as I called them) in their picturesque villages. Belmont, Brinscall, Tockholes, Entwistle; the list was endless. I must explain, for those who do not know, that the term 'readers' refers to the people who borrow books from the Mobile Library. Some librarians call them 'borrowers', but I prefer to call them 'my readers', as to me, at any rate, they weren't just people who came to the van to borrow books – they became my friends whose warmth and generosity of spirit enriched my life every time I met them. In serving their literary needs I found great fulfilment and an empathy of spirit which I shared with them throughout the years. My reverie was interrupted by a loud shriek from outside. I went to investigate and found that Heidi had fallen into a clump of nettles and was trying to nurse her nettled arm and leg at the same time! *"Quick, get some big dock leaves and bring them back here,"* I told Penny, who sped off along the road. Minutes later, Heidi was on my knee, dock leaves on the offending parts whilst I put a tiny ladybird on her hand to distract her attention from the pain. Then: *"Look, a Red Admiral butterfly, the first one of the year,"* I told the girls. She must have just emerged from hibernation and was sunning herself on a pollarded willow in our garden. Heidi looked and was suitably impressed. Pain forgotten, she watched until the beautiful insect fluttered away into the sunshine. *"That's a good girl, I shall make you a chocolate cake for tea,"* I told her as she skipped away to join her sister. I had been reminded that first and foremost I was a wife and mother. And yet, I couldn't wait for my return to the Mobile Library to start. Like a child when a birthday is near, I kept smiling to myself when I thought about it. I could hardly wait to see all my rural friends again.

I'd a whole ten days before I actually started back on the Mobile Library and in every spare minute I found myself thinking about my readers in their charming rural habitats and the picturesque countryside surrounding them. I had been brought up in a grim industrial setting during the Second World War and so it was a delight for me to travel around these beautiful Lancashire villages. I appreciated the scenery as much as the inhabitants.

A myriad of questions flooded my mind. Would there be a lot of new building? Would the villagers still be as friendly and still living where I'd left them? Would they remember me? Would Hull's shop still be there at Brinscall? What about Mrs. Dooley and the vicar's wife at Belmont – would they remember me as I remembered them? I needn't have worried, because in the early 1970s, my Lancashire villages and their residents still retained their unique blend of beauty and charm before the 'Big Brother' towns stretched out their greedy octopus arms to claw and strangle for themselves as much of the countryside as they could.

Living as I did on Rising Bridge Road, just behind me and up Roundhill Lane was the A677 – the Haslingden to Blackburn Road which I knew well as we'd served readers from farms and in cottages and houses who'd lived there.

I thought of Mrs. Whitworth at Ramsclough Farm, old Mr. Whewell at the 'Britannia Inn' and Duckworth Hall and Greenfield Terrace where Mrs. Bates had made us pots of tea on so many occasions in the past. Oh yes, there were many delights in store for me in the near future.

At Rising Bridge, the hawthorn hedges were just beginning to break into that new tender green that I loved so much and two tiny bluetits flirted and fluttered seeking a nest. From my kitchen window I could see the village school where Penny and Heidi were eager pupils. Further to the right stood the village church of St. John's, Stonefold, where we all attended for worship. I gazed with great satisfaction at the lovely green fields and countryside around our house. I heard a lapwing call from a meadow and saw one or two of our neighbours strolling along Rising Bridge Road. The villagers in Rising Bridge, like my Mobile Library villagers, were rather parochial, but they had made us welcome over the years, especially as we had children to swell the ranks of the village church and school.

From my bedroom window, I could see the trees at Carter Place Hall and Height End Hill; scattered with tiny farmhouses and cottages. I stood at the front door to breathe the fresh country air. Magpies chattered from the trees and the smoke from Hollin Gate Cottages plumed its way into the blue sky. The gardens further along the road were a picture of crocuses, aconites and early daffodils blowing in the breeze and winking in the March sunshine. I could have spent all day revelling in the beauty of the Lancashire countryside, knowing that there were many more treats to come when I started my job as Mobile Librarian once more. How I looked forward to that 9am start on Monday morning!

Yippee!

It came at last, a mild spring day with the fields looking very green and inviting, full of new-born lambs as I drove to work through Ewood Bridge and up towards Edenfield, one of my favourite villages. It looked just the same, the very epitome of "England's green and pleasant land" and long may it remain so I thought! As I drove along the main road, I had a wonderful view of Holcombe Hill and Peel Tower up above the little town of Ramsbottom. By 1995, Ramsbottom has become a very 'up-market' town and has expanded rapidly, becoming a great tourist attraction when the branch of the East Lancs Railway re-opened from Bury to Rawtenstall. Ramsbottom has become an overspill town for Manchester. This has brought new business and prosperity to the place, but in the 1970s it was still the same dear, sleepy little town that I'd left some 5 years before. Down through Stubbins I drove and up to the traffic lights, where I turned right into Carr Street, where the new library had been built. The Grant Arms had had a complete facelift, and looked very imposing in the old Market Place. Some of the old shops were still there. I remembered Melvin Crawshaw's the chemist and Rothwell's butchers. At that time, most things were still pretty much in the same mode. Eagerly, I

Ramsbottom, where the Library van, Bill and I were based, seen from Callender Street.

approached the new library building. Yes, there was the Mobile Library waiting outside with Bill smiling and waving at me. Mrs Burch had retired, and now Miss Anna Jackson was Librarian-in-charge. She greeted me warmly and showed me the Mobile Library rota for me to study.

At first glance the routes seemed pretty much the same, with just one or two alterations to the days when we visited different villages and there were quite a few extra places to call at, but I was delighted to see the old familiar names there; Belmont, Edgworth, Tockholes, Withnell, Brinscall, Abbey Village, Entwistle, Hawkshaw, Affetside, Egerton, Belthorn, Dimple, Green Haworth, just a few of the names of places I longed to see again. Bill was happy to see me and said he'd told many of my old friends who'd borrowed books from the Mobile Library of my return. Apparently, many of them would be as glad to see me as I was to see them, he told me as I settled into the front seat of the cab. This new van was slightly larger than our older one, and had a locker for my bags and belongings. *"First stop today is Round Barn at Entwistle,"* Bill told me, and I could hardly wait to see the lovely countryside and reservoirs on the way to this picturesque row of cottages.

We're off!!

Out of Ramsbottom we trundled, through Holcombe Brook and Hawkshaw, with the tiny gardens bright with crocuses and snowdrops. We reached the Bull's Head and turned right towards Edgworth. I looked around in delight, revelling in the beauty surrounding me and the old familiar features; St. Anne's Church at Turton, Chapeltown Road winding towards Bromley Cross, the green fields and

12

hills, and in the background, the majesty of Winter Hill with tiny Belmont Village nestling at his feet. Some twenty years later, at the time of writing, the landscape has changed considerably. The Jumbles reservoir has been created, and from Bromley Cross, large estates of new houses reach all along parts of Chapeltown Road. In the early 1970s, both Bromley Cross and Harwood libraries still belonged to the Ramsbottom region, and we visited both branches quite regularly.

Anyway, on this bright March morning, we coasted down the road and up to Edgworth village then on towards Entwistle. I glanced round as we passed by the Edgworth Post Office, and on the opposite side of the road was the famous Holden's Ice-cream shop, still selling that deliciously special concoction of their own making (so Bill told me). He and I caught up on the news and changes in our lives as we travelled towards Round Barn. The pretty cottages at Hob Lane were as lovely as ever, with yellow forsythia frothing around the walls and fences, and their front gardens a riot of polyanthus and primula denticulata ('drumstick primula' as it is more commonly known). Down the dip in the road we sped, past Jimmy the Postman's cottage and up to Round Barn admiring the beautiful Entwistle scenery. No Scottish loch or hillside setting could have looked more lovely. Further up the road was the Crown and Thistle pub where we turned round.

It was roughly the same routine as before. Bill sounded the horn, and almost at once the tiny doors opened. Two or three little women with piles of books in their arms rushed to the van door. I opened it and stood there smiling, waiting. Would they remember me or not? First to reach the door was Mrs. Molloy, a diminutive figure with a scarf round her head to protect her newly permed grey hair. *"Why, Mrs. Moore, how nice to see you again,"* she exclaimed. *"It's good to be back, I've missed this part of the world so much,"* I told her. We chatted as

Ramsbottom

I exchanged her books and two other readers left theirs to be discharged. One of them smiled briefly, and I recognised her as Mrs. Walton who used to bring her two babies to the library van. *"Yes, they're both at Hob Lane School now,"* she said in answer to my enquiry. Mrs. Molloy brought us two cups of coffee and told me who'd been 'hatched, matched and dispatched' since my absence. Not much had changed, as is usual in the rural areas where the pace of life is so much slower. How wonderful it was to sit, drinking the coffee and be able to enjoy the countryside around me.

Darwen Tower twinkled in the March sunshine, robins were carolling to their mates, and far below, sunbeams danced on the waters of the reservoirs like golden diamonds. The dark green of the conifer and pine trees contrasted with the tender young shoots of new grass and foxgloves, which would burst into glorious colour in June. My heart rejoiced with all the lovely gifts that Lancashire had to offer.

Under Attack.

Leaving Round Barn behind, we visited Rook Farm, where a new borrower, Mrs. Haydock, lived with her collection of animals. Bill told me she was famous locally for her special healing powers with animals and birds, and that people often came to her rather than send for the vet. Mrs. Haydock was rosy cheeked and wrinkled, with grey wispy hair and thin steel rimmed glasses, behind which her brilliant blue eyes twinkled inquisitively. **When** she had time to read, she told me, she liked country books and historical novels. As we were leaving, a collection of assorted geese and ducks waddled into the farmyard and began to forage round the library van. *"Time to go,"* said Bill and sounded the horn. The birds took no notice. He tried again; louder this time. Still no response; in fact, they crowded round us even more. Mrs. Haydock tried to shoo them away, but to no avail! I shouted at them from the open door of the Library van, and the geese reared up and made menacing hissing noises, eyeing me malevolently all the while. I hastily dodged back into the van. The geese made a lunge for Mrs. Haydock and she quickly put distance between herself and them. Geese and ducks surged round the van once more, rooting and poking into the ground round the wheels.

Whatever it was they were after certainly held their aggressive attention. Time was getting on, we were already late for the next stop, but how could we remove the offending birds without running over at least some of them?

Mrs. Haydock went round the back of the barn and appeared with a long plastic hosepipe. *"This will move them, just you watch,"* she said. A fierce stream of water shot forth with such velocity that the birds were lifted off the ground and spun round like whirligigs, the geese tumbling backwards. They soon made a quick retreat back to their field. I laughed at the sight of the birds being dispatched so neatly, and after thanking Mrs. Haydock, we drove off quickly to make up for lost time. *"I wonder what they were after?"* asked Bill. *"I don't know. Remind me to ask Mrs. Haydock next time,"* I replied.

14

Back towards Edgworth we trundled, calling at several more houses on the way. We turned down Hob Lane and I noticed with delight the hawthorn hedges, a flurry of verdant green tipping their dark branches. Over the Wayoh reservoir we went, and I looked across the blue waters towards Edgworth and the Methodist Church spire which graced the skyline. Up we went, past Mrs. Simpson's tea gardens which were not yet open, past old Entwistle Hall where Mary Jepson of the famous 'Jepson's of Darwen' tripe used to live, and round by the Entwistle station where I'd got stuck in the loo some years earlier. The Strawbury Duck pub had had a facelift and looked very smart.

We waited at the corner of Edge Lane for the usual crowd of readers to attend from Railway Terrace and the surrounding farms. Yes, I recognised several old faces and they recognised me too. We exchanged greetings and old Mrs. Jackson told me she now had 10 great-grandchildren and a new Tabby cat. Mopsey, the one she'd had when I was last here had died at the ripe old age of 15. Then we drove along Railway Terrace, as it was then because it was near the station. Later it became Overshores Road and was closed to traffic, but at that time we could drive along it to reach Harry Jolley's bungalow. He was Water Bailiff at that time and I envied him his wonderful views both at the front and rear of his house. As we drew up outside Harry's gate, a grey squirrel which had been eating from his bird table took a huge leap across the overflow and fled into the woods. Harry greeted me warmly and said that a great number of pine trees had been planted since I'd left.

Edgworth's Barlow Institute and Recreation Ground are at the centre of village life.

15

The 'Strawbury Duck' is an unusual name, with an unusual spelling, in an unusual, difficult to find, location - but well worth a visit.

Fresh Air Dining.

Dinner was eaten at the other side of Entwistle Reservoir overlooking the emerald waters and I could see two coots busily seeking nesting material at one side. I sighed with contentment as I enjoyed salad sandwiches and orange juice, then took a brief walk along one of the little lanes. In 1996 there are car parks for people to leave their vehicles by the side of the reservoir so that they can enjoy walking, but in the 1970s, the paths were still open to walkers and there were far fewer cars.

After lunch we turned onto Greens Arms Road which links the A666 Blackburn to Bolton road with Turton Village. I was looking forward to meeting some of my old readers. I wasn't disappointed either – there they were, large as life, just as homely and friendly as I'd remembered them, especially Mrs. Rose Rogers who was an expert at spinning and weaving. Then it was down Chapeltown Road, where Mrs. Woods made us coffee as usual. In fact, at the time of writing in 1996, she is still making coffee for the Mobile Library staff. What a wonderful record of goodwill she has. She was as pleased to see me back again as I was to see her. We had a busy afternoon serving more houses and some farms in the area, then it was back to Ramsbottom for 5pm.

"Did you enjoy yourself?" asked Miss Anna as I slipped a pile of request slips onto the library counter. *"I most certainly did,"* I replied, *"I can't wait for*

each new day to enjoy meeting my old friends and making new ones." Miss Anna smiled at me and I headed for Rising Bridge.

The Fortnightly Cycle.

It was a wonderful two weeks for me, for the Mobile Library ran a fortnightly schedule, so I was reunited with my readers old and new for the first time in five years. The routes were pretty much the same as when I'd last worked on them, with a few new places like Hoddlesden, Withnell Fold and the new parts of Belthorn being included. At the end of two weeks when we'd completed a full cycle of routes, I felt like I'd never been away at all. True, there had been some building during my absence, but at that time the villages still maintained their own special features and charm, before the towns overspilled into them and stole away the countryside around them. Writing in 1996, I'm very surprised at the amount of building there has been since the early 1970s. The Chapeltown Road area and Bromley Cross, for instance, have been altered tremendously. Still, people need houses and it hadn't altered the kind nature of most of my readers, I reflected optimistically. The girls had settled in at St. John's Stonefold School, Gordon was enjoying his work and I looked forward to many more years serving my friends 'the readers' with the Mobile Library. I was back home again as a true 'Lancashire Native'.

APRIL MAGIC: GREEN HILLS NOT SO FAR AWAY

April has always been a special month for me and this particular year was no exception. As the days advanced, so did the greening of the Lancashire countryside. The delicate green of the hawthorn was blending with the bright yellow of the forsythia and the first tender new leaves of the pussy willows. Village gardens sported large clumps of white rock and aubretia which would be in full flower later and the polyanthus gave way to the velvety faces of the pansies. My heart delighted in this new awakening of the earth after its long winter sleep, and I knew I'd have a lot to look forward to and enjoy.

It was a wonderful spring day towards the middle of April when we left Ramsbottom for the Brinscall area, one of my favourite library trips. Passing through Hawkshaw, the gardens were alive and cheery with violas, grape hyacinths, daffodils and tulips. Spring always came relatively late to our little area of North East Lancashire, but the ensuing glory of blossoming plants and flowering shrubs made the wait worthwhile. Little Miss Martin was busy weeding and brushing the path of her immaculate cottage, and she waved her trowel at us as we coasted past. Down towards Bradshaw we cruised, where the old-fashioned clock of the Parish Church steadily ticked away the passage of time as it had done for so many years. Mr. Bolton, a local farmer was delivering milk with his old horse Polly in the shafts of his wooden milk-cart. *"He must be one of the last people to be delivering milk by horse,"* I told Bill.

Soon we were passing through Egerton and heading towards Longworth Lane where we turned left for Belmont Village, passing through the Belmont Bleaching and Dyeing Company's factory buildings. What a lovely day! The green green fields, fresh with morning dew sparkled like diamonds. Lambs frisked round and teased their placid mothers, gaining strength every day and rejoicing in their new-found freedom. How lucky I was to have a job where I could see so much of our bounteous Lancashire countryside.

The spire of St. Peter's Church, Belmont, became visible, and as we dived down the dip through the Bleaching and Dyeing Company, a skull and crossbones proclaimed 'Death around the corner' in order to reduce speed on a bad bend. Up Belmont High Street, past the old Post Office and Maria Square we trundled. Several of the elderly villagers, oil-cloth bags and wicker shopping baskets on their arms were heading for the Co-op store which was a popular local gossip shop. The April sky was blue as sapphires and the moorland air sweet as wine. Fresh vibrant shoots

18

St.Peter's Church, Belmont, stands on a rise above the main road. The churchyard's residents could not have a more peaceful resting place.

of bracken and fern were mingling with and usurping last year's growths as we coasted along the moorland road and a kestrel flew across in front of the Library van. The road to Tockholes turned invitingly to the right, but that was not our destination on this day. Roddlesworth Reservoir gleamed on our right and soon the Hare and Hounds pub at Abbey Village hove in view. We didn't need to sound the horn as several readers were already waiting at the first stop, chattering and exchanging news as we pulled into the side of the road. I smiled with pleasure as I welcomed these my friends and readers aboard. A unanimous chorus greeted me. *"Morning Mrs. Moore, nice to see you and what a lovely day."* Two infants rushed up with their mother, just as we were about to tidy up before we left for the next stop. *"Sorry,"* called a breathless Sally Halton; *"we've called at Lily Marsden's toffee shop, that's why we're a bit late."* I smiled indulgently at the two rosy-cheeked cherubs choosing a new library book. Lily Marsden's shop was never ever empty or short of customers. The weaving mill was still running then, providing employment for villagers.

Off we trundled up the A675 Bolton Road and past the quaint little houses, all with different coloured doors which winked and shone in the April sunshine, their paint work and steps gleaming with cleanliness and the care bestowed on them by their hard-working owners. In the playground of the village school, the children whooped and skipped, danced and frisked as merrily as the lambs we'd just seen, enjoying their freedom and the April freshness.

A Well-Baked Tart

Down through Abbey Village we made our way, stopping in several different places for the convenience of our readers who were elderly or infirm. They welcomed us with open arms. As there were far, far fewer cars and televisions in those days of the early 1970s, there weren't as many distractions. No falling 'issues' here – we did 700 to 800 issues each time we visited this little community, and people really enjoyed their books – you could tell by the comments they made to me later. Mrs. Hill brought us a cup of coffee and a piece of her delicious Bakewell Tart. Dear readers, always so kind and welcoming, how I looked forward to seeing them every fortnight.

Eating Greens amongst the Greenery

At the northern edge of the village, we turned round and drove back towards Bolton, turning off to the right at Dole Lane on our way to visit Withnell. I noticed a few swallows skimming in and out of some old barns and I marvelled once more at the ability of a tiny bird like that to fly almost 6000 miles across land and sea, right back to its birthplace in Lancashire. I could see the unusual spire of St. Paul's Church, Withnell, in the distance across the fields. Marie Hoole's shop was a popular stop at the bottom of Bury Lane, and soon we were inundated with readers, books and baskets, plastic carriers and string bags as piles of books were exchanged and discharged.

Old Dick Hartley, who was all but stone deaf, tried to tell me what he wanted above the babble of various conversations taking place in the Library van. *"Ah wants a nanimal book,"* he roared. *"Mi pigs 'ave getten green spots,"* he asserted. I looked in vain for a veterinary book. *"Nothing suitable here, sorry, but if you like, I can take a request for one next time."* Just then, Ned Grundy who'd heard the conversation butted in. *"What 'ave you been feeding 'em on Dick?"* *"Well, mash, scraps, meal, left over veg and plenty of cabbage, why?"* *"Tha gormless divil, tha's given 'em too many greens an' that's why thiv getten green spots,"* owd Ned replied and laughed heartily. Whether he meant this or not I'll never know, as Dick stormed out of the van in a huff as everyone joined in the fun.

We continued up Bury Lane along to Bracken Farm where the barn had been converted into two cottages. In one of them lived Maud and Alice Turner, two spinster sisters. Sometimes they came to choose books together and at other times they came separately. This morning only Miss Maud appeared. She informed us that Alice had a bad cold and that she would be choosing some books for her. *"Silly beggar, hoo never put her hairnet on when shi went to church last week. No wonder shi's getten a cowd in her head,"* muttered Maud. I wondered vaguely what protection against cold would a hairnet be, but I refrained from pointing this out. Miss Maud zoomed round the shelves like an angry wasp, picking up first one book and then another and flinging them down in disgust, clacking her false teeth together like an agitated hen. *"Have you nothing with a bit of life in it?"* she grumbled. Rather taken aback by her obvious contempt for my book stock, I asked mildly: *"What kind of life?"* *"Well, you know, one with a bit o' true romance, strange affairs and plenty o' sex,"* Maud replied, rolling her eyes heavenward and dislodging her clacking teeth in the process. I looked at the bent, wizened figure and scrawny hand and pinched face, wondering how she knew what sex and affairs were all about. Still, I was there to help, so I produced two or three raunchy, modern novels for her to choose from. In the end she decided to take them all and I imagined her sat up in bed toothless, with hairnet on her head and scrawny hand poised to eagerly turn over the page for the next lurid affair or sweltering account of a sexual encounter. As I closed the door behind her, Bill remarked: *"We get some rum old birds in here don't we?"* I nodded in agreement and we went on our way.

To the Woods.

Sometimes, especially in winter, we had our dinner at the little café on the A675 Belmont Road, at the corner opposite the Hoghton Arms. But today was so lovely, that I persuaded Bill to trundle down to Lodge Bank at Brinscall where I could go for a walk in the woods. I saw two coots nesting and a shy moorhen's nest amongst the reeds, and I shared my left-over bits of crumbs with a bevy of mallards and Barnacle geese who followed me round as I walked. Then it was up the path and into Brinscall woods, where the enchantment of April's magic really enfolded and delighted me. I wandered aimlessly, enjoying the sound of robins and blackbirds carolling in sweet delight. A tiny wren bobbed to me and then dived into a hollow tree.

A Glimpse of Paradise.

I walked into the glade and gasped in sheer delight – it was so beautiful. Tiny golden celandines, like tumbled sunbeams smiled up at me from the damp, moist floor. Wood anemones, delicate as flakes of snow trembled and danced on their slender stalks, like so many ballerinas. I caught the faint smell of violets, and, amongst the tree roots, I discovered a few of these precious little flowers. A few pale primroses gemmed the banks by the stream and I could scent ransoms or 'garlic plant' as it is more commonly known. I sat on a fallen tree and imbibed the wonders of this lovely spot, rejoicing in its beauty and freshness, and the joy it gave me. Then, the ultimate! The triumphant call of the cuckoo, newly returned from his winter shores, echoed around the glade and woods, breaking the stillness and adding its own poignant beauty to the atmosphere. The cuckoo's call roused me from my reverie and reminded me that I still had half a day's work to complete and that my readers would be waiting. Reluctantly I tore myself away from that heavenly spot and walked back to where Bill was waiting for me. Just a brief glimpse of paradise, but it will remain forever in my memory as one of the loveliest spots I'd ever seen.

Off we went back up to the corner of Bett Lane at Higher Wheelton, where our first batch of readers would be waiting for us. The lilac trees in Mrs. Grundy's garden were in bud, and her old tabby cat was stretched out on the windowsill, basking in the April sunshine. Mrs. Grundy greeted me cheerfully; *"Warming-up, isn't it? Soon be time for bedding plants and hanging baskets,"* she asserted. Jack

Moss joined in the conversation. *"Got some lovely calendulas and begonias ready to plant out – best I've ever propagated. You can have some if you like when you're ready,"* he told Mrs. Grundy, who beamed delightedly.

Mrs. Fairburn, A Bunny Girl.

Further up the lane, at Oakwood Cottages, was Mrs. Fairburn, a delightful reader who reminded me of Little Grey Rabbit, because of her long, grey, flannel coat, which covered her ample bosom. With her pink, flabby cheeks and piles of grey hair protruding high above her 80 year old head. She looked so innocent and cherubic that she appeared almost childlike. She had been a District Nurse locally, and often recounted amusing tales and anecdotes about her job to anyone who cared to listen. Bill and myself were eager to be recipients of these amusing anecdotes, and Mrs. Fairburn never failed to tell us something new on each visit.

Today was no exception. She told us about an over-agitated father to be who broke every piece of his wife's treasured tea-set because he crashed into the display-cabinet, so anxious was he to run next door for the neighbours when his wife went into labour.

Beautiful Brinscall.

Up Bett Lane we went to where it changed its name to Buckholes Brow, where we had two farms to visit and where the readers were very appreciative of our services. Then we continued to rise until we came to the top of School Lane and I saw the village of Brinscall spread below me. I remembered how I'd felt the first time I'd seen this same scene when I'd started back at my job on the Mobile Library after an absence of five years, and I'd paid my first visit to this dear little community hoping that it was still the same as when I'd left it earlier. A lump came into my throat as we crested the top of School Lane and I saw the houses and gardens of Brinscall stretched out before me.

No, it hadn't changed, not at all and silly me – I didn't want it to. Nor the dear warm-hearted disarming inhabitants who'd given me so much pleasure and taken me to their hearts years ago.

When I see today's world full of plastic cards and mendacious rubbish, I can't help feeling we've changed for the worse. So many of the old Lancashire traditions and customs which were part of our heritage have been swept away by administrators with no thought for the ordinary people. The people here in this little moorland community were my Lancashire readers, my rural Lancashire natives and I wouldn't have them changed, no – not if I could help it.

I ran down School Lane whilst readers were choosing their books, eager to satisfy my hopes and longings. Yes, it was still the same! The Post Office, the butcher's, Hull's grocers and the dear little cottages and houses lining each side of the road where my readers had lived and worked and generally carried-on their lives as their ancestors had done before them. I felt comforted to know that this little community and its typical Lancashire natives had managed to retain their own particular brand of rural Lancashire life in the face of so-called 'Progress'.

'The lodge', which is a sparkling little area of water behind the baths at the bottom of the village of Brinscall, never failed to amaze me with its wide variety of birds, some of whom nested there all the year round, and others like the Canada geese who only visited in the winter. I saw mallards, coots, moorhens, herons, Canada and Barnacle geese, swans and, once, a small crested grebe, all happily splashing about and diving under the surface of that little lodge which was a haven for other wildlife.

Brinscall was unusual as well in that it had its own Public Baths, which are still of great benefit to the community at large and to the children in particular. The baths were next to the lodge, so in the school holidays, I often saw the children come straight out from the baths and go to look at the birds on the lodge. The birds were certainly well-fed judging by the amount of bread I saw handed out to them. The children of Brinscall and district were very lucky to be brought up in such a lovely environment.

A Bath at Brinscall.

One rather cool day in mid-June, I was walking round the lodge taking note of the new chicks and late arrivals of the mallards and coots, when one of the ducks began making a terrible noise. I looked round and saw a tiny duckling being swept towards the overflow which was just behind me. The poor duckling was powerless against the sweeping current and mother was frantically trying to save it, but could do nothing!

I realised there was no time to loose, so throwing off my shoes and rolling up my skirt, I plunged into the water at the other side of the overflow where it wasn't

The Lodge bank, Brinscall, on a March day.

23

quite so deep. I was just in time to catch the luckless duckling as it tipped over the edge of the water, the mother still making a terrible noise at the back of it. Now I had to launch the duckling back into the lodge near its mother, so I climbed onto the wooden ledge of the overflow and walked across to the other side, the mother squawking in terror as she watched me with her baby. Again I walked into the water, the duckling in my hand ready to launch it next to mother. I put my hands down and let go of the tiny bird, but mother duck must have thought I was harming it, and the silly bird lunged forward and gave me a vicious peck on the wrist which caused me to lose my balance and fall forward with an almighty splash into the cool water! I emerged gasping for breath and looking a sorry sight with pond weed and mud dripping down my face. I spluttered and coughed as I scrambled towards the bank, with the malicious duck cackling at the side of me, for all the world as if she were laughing at my plight, not a bit grateful that I'd rescued her offspring!

I stood on the bank wondering what to do next, as Bill was in the van up School Lane and knew nothing of my adventure. I shook myself like a dog and looked around me, feeling very sorry for myself as I couldn't serve the afternoon readers in all those wet clothes.

I'd just decided to go into the baths for a clean-up, when I heard a shout from the garden of one of the houses along Lodge Bank. It was Mrs. Linda Haworth, one of our most avid readers and, unknown to me, she'd seen the whole episode. She hurried towards me full of concern, but as she got nearer and saw what a sight I looked, she couldn't contain her laughter, and in the end, neither could I!

I was dripping mud, water and weed all over the road by now. *"Come to my house and have a bath – that'll get rid of all the mud and weed,"* she exclaimed. I murmured my thanks and followed her to her lovely home on Lodge Bank. *"But what about my clothes – I've nothing to wear?"* Mrs. Haworth took charge of everything. *"Come into the kitchen and take everything off; you can put them all in a plastic dustbin bag and I'll lend you some old clothes of mine,"* she urged me, *"then you can have a bath. Where are your shoes by the way?"* she asked. *"Damn! I've left them by the overflow,"* I said. Actually it gave me such a shock falling in the cold water, that I'd forgotten about my shoes and hadn't even felt the hard road.

"No!" Mrs. Haworth was quite adamant. *"You take your clothes off in the kitchen and put this towel round you, and I'll get your shoes."* She was out of the door before I could protest, so I peeled off my soaking garments and put them in the bin bag, wrapped myself in the warm bath towel and sat down on a kitchen chair. Mrs. Haworth bounced in, my shoes and socks in her hand. *"Silly birds, they were still messing about near the overflow – you'd think they'd have more sense, wouldn't you?"* she remarked. I was still smarting from the impromptu ducking! *"Last time I'll rescue anything for any more birds; they never learn, do they?"* Mrs. Haworth nodded sympathetically, *"I'll make you a cup of tea when you come down,"* she said as she ushered me upstairs. What bliss to slip into the warm, scented water and wash the mud and weed from my face and hair. I mustn't linger too long though, as Bill would be wondering where I was.

View from the bottom of School Lane, Brinscall, March 1995.

Reluctantly, I left the comfort of the bathroom and found that Mrs. Haworth had put a complete set of clothes outside the door for me. Luckily we were roughly the same size, so I didn't look too bad in a lavender blouse and black skirt. My shoes, of course, were quite dry, which was a blessing. I enjoyed the strong, hot cup of tea which was waiting for me in the kitchen. *"Thank you very much; you've been so kind,"* I told Linda.

"Not at all," she replied, *"I'm glad to have been of use. Bring my clothes back on your next visit; I don't need them until then,"* she told me. *"Oh, by the way – keep away from ducks in future!"* Linda smiled as I ran round the corner into School Lane where the Mobile Library was waiting for me.

Bill was astonished to see me return in different clothes from the ones I'd left him in. *"What's happened?"* he queried, noting my damp hair and lavender blouse, instead of a pink one. But there was no time to explain as our readers at the first of the afternoon stops were already mounting the steps of the van. *"I'll tell you later,"* I mouthed at Bill as we hastily discharged their books. Yet it was not to be, because Ken Riding and his wife, Elsie, who ran the local fish'n'chip shop at the bottom of School Lane had also witnessed the drama.

It was funny really, because Ken originally came from the Accrington area and I was quite friendly with him in the 1950s. However, he'd married Elsie, a girl from Brinscall and went to live in that community. They ran the local chip shop from the early 1970s and, in fact, still do in 1996. He was not slow to poke fun at my plight, still remembering the ribbings I'd given him during our teenage years.

"Well, well, it's the little mermaid today, is it?" he joked. *"I saw you rise from the lodge like the Loch Ness Monster itself,"* he continued. *"What were you*

doing, anyway?" enquired Elsie.

I blushed as I looked round and saw that all the readers were hanging on every word that Ken and Elsie had said, and were now waiting for a suitable reply or explanation from me. I began haltingly, then I laughed and told them the full tale. They were entitled to a bit of excitement at my expense, I decided; heaven knows I'd had many a laugh with them in the past.

There were suitable commiserations after I'd finished telling them about the accident, and one or two of the older men clacked their teeth and said that *"Them ducks is so stupid, its a wonder any ducklings survived at all."* *"We could put some wire netting across the overflow to prevent any more tragedies,"* observed Jim Turner. *"Yes, that's a good idea,"* several other readers chorused in unison. *"Will you see to it, Jim?"* He promised to do just that. I was quite recovered and warm and dry now, so I popped into Hull's shop which sold all manner of wonderful delicacies as well as the basic things that the villagers needed. Tom Murphy was behind the counter. *"Hello, Mrs. Moore, what can I do for you today?"*

Tommy's eyes were kind and gentle as I ordered my goodies. He served the villagers of Brinscall and Withnell very well until the shop closed in 1990 and I still call to see him at his home on Chapel Street.

Up School Lane we continued, past the Post Office and St. Joseph's Catholic Club. *"What super little houses these are – like the ones in Bury Lane, Withnell,"* I remarked to Bill. My readers kept them clean and spotless, taking great pride in both the inside and outside on equal terms.

Mrs. Kath Watson, the postlady hailed us from across the road. *"Can you wait just two minutes, please – I'd forgotten it was your week, so I need to go home for the family's books."* I nodded agreement and began to tidy the shelves while we waited for her. Minutes later, a breathless Mrs. Watson clambered into the van. *"Thanks very much for waiting,"* she began. *"Oh, and by the way, did you know that Mrs. Gerrard has died? She used to get books from you, didn't she? Has she any out at the moment?"* I looked up, surprised by her news. *"No, I didn't know she'd died, and yes, she has four books of ours. What shall I do about getting them back?"* I asked Kath Watson. *"Leave it to me. I'll see her daughter and get them back for you for the next visit,"* she promised. *"You're very kind,"* I murmured. *"Well, so are you – waiting for me like that,"* said Kath. Such were the courtesies and pleasantries that we exchanged, librarian and readers in happy harmony.

ALL THINGS BRIGHT AND BEAUTIFUL, ALL READERS GREAT AND SMALL

I have always thought that May is one of the loveliest months of the year, when the awakening of the earth culminates in plant and animal life beginning a resurgence of their beauty. Birds are feeding nestlings, the lilac trees, their buds caressed by the soft rain, finally open and their perfume wafts over the gardens and churchyards. Everything around seems fresh and new as the hawthorn whitens the hedgerows, the blossom contrasting sharply with that special green of the new hawthorn leaves. At least, that's how I saw it when I was working on the Mobile Library and indeed, 25 years later, I still eagerly await the coming of May and always will do.

May Day

On this particular May 1st (it wasn't a Bank Holiday then) the day dawned warm and sunny. As I drove down Ewood Bridge towards Edenfield, I looked to the right where the little community of Irwell Vale and its delightful chapel twinkled in the May sunshine. Driving up through Edenfield, I glanced at Musbury Tor, Helmshore's famous hill, his majestic head a crown of deep new green. Further along was Holcombe Hill, a vibrant shade of emerald, basking in the morning sun. How beautiful they are, these eternal Lancashire landmarks. I saw the spire of Holcombe Parish Church and the dark cluster of houses which composed the village around it. Oh yes, Lancashire has so many beautiful places if only people will stop and take time to look at them. I drove down through Stubbins where the Irwell wends its gleaming way and so eventually into Carr Street, Ramsbottom, where the Mobile Library awaited me. Soon we were winging along towards Edgworth and Broadfield Road; my heart rejoicing at the beauty of the tiny country gardens full of pansies, primulas, cherry trees and late daffodils. Our first port of call was at 'Witches Den', the home of Miss Letitia Longbottom. a marvellous old lady in whom I'd taken a special interest when I first started on the Mobile Library in the 1960s.

She was noted for her gushing expressions which endeared her to me as I only saw her once every two weeks. Her neighbours were not so keen. Sure enough, Miss Letitia bounced into the van and commented; *"What a lovely day isn't it? And how are those darling children of yours and your dear husband? Are they all well?"* These questions were all fired at me so quickly that I couldn't separate

27

them. I opened my mouth to reply, but Miss Letitia spoke again. *"Do please find me some more of those adorable 'Miss Read' books, sweetie,"* she gushed, (as her eyesight was bad I had to choose some Large Print books for her) I duly obliged, whilst Miss Letitia wittered on about the weather, the world, politics and anything else her scatty brain could think of. She was a dear, though rather lonely, so I indulged her little whims. At length, Miss Letitia was satisfied and, pulling her mauve cardigan tightly round her chest, departed back to her little cottage.

The sun shone even more brightly as the day progressed. We saw one or two horses bedecked with ribbons and their tails plaited as was the custom on May Day many years ago. Even though we were touring a rural area, there were not as many people who adhered to these old traditions and customs as there used to be. I wondered if we'd see any Maypoles round the villages, as this was another old English custom which was fast dying out. I knew that my own two little girls were going with the Stonefold Brownies to dance round their Maypole in Hoyle, Belgrave and Hazel Streets in Rising Bridge in order to raise money for our local church, St. John's, Stonefold, as well as enjoying themselves. They then took the Maypole to Acre and down Hud Hey Road, then back along Rising Bridge Road to the church, stopping and dancing at strategic places, all taking turns to be the May Queen and proffering the church collection tin. We did see quite a few Maypoles on our rounds, although they were mostly in schoolyards, where the children danced around the Maypole at the same time as having a lesson in Country Dancing.

28

We drove over Broadhead Road and past Winwards' and other farms, but it wasn't their turn for the Mobile Library on this day. It was so lovely, the sky a forget-me-not blue with fluffy clouds like dabs of cotton wool floating round. A rook loomed overhead and I heard a curlew's warbles as he scoured the moors looking for prey. Dinner was eaten at the Grey Mare, and the landlord gave us each a glass of lemonade to accompany our sandwiches. There wasn't anywhere near as much 'eating out' in those days, as there were fewer cafés and the pubs weren't serving food then.

We left the Grey Mare behind and coasted down towards Guide where we had to make a right turn to Oswaldtwistle. But before we reached School Lane, we had a call to make at a small detached house with a large garden and allotment at the back. This was the home of Miss Ethel Winterbotham. What a good name it was for her! As she hadn't been one of my former readers and had moved to the area when I was working elsewhere, I didn't know her, and what a shock I got the first time I met her. A scraggy old lady of about 70 years of age, her grey hair frizzed out from her head in spikes, looking just like icicles. Her fiercely cold blue eyes gleamed maliciously behind thin, old-fashioned wire spectacles and she didn't miss a thing! As I got used to seeing her, she appeared less fierce, but her dour looks and sharp tongue meant that I couldn't chat with her as with my other readers. I'd never heard her speak pleasantly in all the time we called on her, and this day was no exception. Bill tooted the horn and she appeared at the house door, slamming it behind her so forcefully that the house shook to its very foundations.

"Hello, Miss Winterbottom," as soon as I opened my mouth I realised I'd made a mistake. *"Winterbotham, Woman!!"* she bawled at me, an emphasis on the *"...tham"*. Suitably chastised, I left her to flounce round the van whilst I did some office work. Bill tried to ease the tension by recommending a new Dick Francis to her. But Miss Ethel was not to be smoothed over after my unfortunate pronouncement and paid no heed to either of us. I knew she liked murders and wasn't really surprised, as I was sure she could kill someone with the look in her eye if she chose to do so. *"Well, that's it! Nothing much here today,"* she snapped as the books were slammed on the table to have the tickets taken out. She stormed out of the door without even a nod. *"Frosty old faggot,"* I said to Bill. *"As dry as a wrinkled prune,"* he countered. *"I'll bet she doesn't know what a good loving is; it would do her good."* Bill gave me a conspiratorial wink and we rumbled on towards School Lane and the Britannia Inn crossroads with the A677 to Haslingden where we turned right.

Observing Ossie.

I enjoyed that lovely drive. We called at several farmhouses and cottages near Ye Olde Brown Cow Inn, including Red Shell Lane, New Moss Farm and the famous Holding's Pottery on the left. Below, sleepy Oswaldtwistle lay drowsing in the May sunshine. I could see familiar landmarks as I'd spent my childhood there. The spires of Immanuel and Holy Trinity churches could be seen above the haze of green created by the new leaves. Rhyddings Mill chimney and that of Stanhill Ring Spinning Mill (which was demolished in 1985) were proudly proclaiming the last remnants of Lancashire's cotton industry. I didn't know it then, but later, I was to work in Oswaldtwistle Library for quite a few years, my first published book being about the people of that friendly little town. On that glorious May afternoon, the moors above Oswaldtwistle were a picture. Fresh new bracken interspersed with rough moorland scrub and the gorse bushes were a haven for wildlife. From the meadows near Bumper Hall Farm, two larks rose into the rainbowed sky and sang joyously, soaring in ecstasy. A heron coasted by, on his way to one of the reservoirs towards Town Bent, Waterside and Hoyle Bottom. As we approached the Coach and Horses Inn, I could see Childer's Farm and Benjamin Row in the small valley below.

Benjamin Row is a small number of cottages reached from the road past Green Haworth Chapel and by turning right down the farm track. At one time it was a very popular port of call for walkers, as big white jugs of tea could be bought there for a few pennies. I can remember as a child at Easter time hiking to Benjamin Row, eating my sandwiches and enjoying swigs of tea from the huge jug. Now, very few hikers call at the cottages.

Mrs. Whitworth at Ramsclough Farm showed me several swallows' nests in her various out buildings and I was very interested to see several of these marvellous little birds flying in and out of barn doors to feed their nestlings. What a wonderful brain those tiny birds must have. *"How do they do it?"* I asked Mrs. Whitworth, but she was no wiser than I.

The Fields of the Cloth of Gold.

Leaving Ramsclough Farm behind, we headed along the A677 and turned right at Broadfield to reach Cross Edge and Green Haworth. As we manoeuvred round, I suddenly grabbed Bill's hand and let out a shriek of delight. *"Stop, stop. Please stop,"* I shouted. *"Whatever's the matter?"* asked Bill, slamming on the brakes and pulling into the side of the road. I pointed to the fields across the road and he saw what I meant. There, in the corner meadow, stretching as far as I could see was a patch of gold; pure gold, real gold. 'Poor man's gold' I called it, the only gold that mattered to me! I jumped out of the van and ran across the road to the meadow and gazed wonderingly at the blaze of golden marsh marigolds, basking in the May sunshine.

What a lovely sight! The marsh marigolds were interspersed by clumps of Lady's Smocks – sometimes called 'Cuckoo Flower' or more commonly 'May Flower', their delicate lavender colour blending sweetly with the green of the meadow and the gold of the flowers. To add to my delight, two tiny lambs left their mother up the top of the field and came frisking towards me, curious to see who this silly person was. I gave them some bits of apple I had left over and they crunched them appreciatively. My daughters call me 'soppy and old fashioned' because I love flowers and Lancashire's green countryside so much. *"Let them say what they will,"* I thought as the shimmering yellow dazzled my eyes. *"They don't know what they are missing."* Reluctantly I left the marsh marigolds and the lambs

30

T' Swallas 'ev Landed Brindle
by Michael May

"T' swallas 'ev landed Brindle," Ah wer towd bi mi mate Harry,
An' them few simple words o' 'is, set mi thowts o' in a flurry,
Ah wondered 'ow many t'seasons wor them swallas 'ev landed back,
Five, er 'appen ten thahsand yeer? Er is it moor than that?

Wor thi even cummin' 'ere wen Brindle Æeden't a name,
Wi' nowt but forrest abaht, afoor any fooak came,
An' wod is it abaht Brindle, that gi's it such a poo,
As them swallas, just t'get 'ere, six thahsand mile 'ev flew?

Thi'v cum frae t'sahth of Africa, weer its gettin' winter theer,
An' nah ther flyin' rahnd Brindle Church, caus its early springtime 'ere.
'Ow duh thi know just weer t'cum? Ah'm sure its not bi chance,
These swallas knows just weer t'part frae them as lives i' France.

T'Lord alone knows 'ow thi cross them dangerous lonely skies,
Wi' nowt but tiny swept-back wings, an' eytin' nowt but flies,
An' 'ow many is ther missin' aht o' them that swoop an' dive,
As med that trip that many times thi couldn't manage t' survive?

Wor thi wingin' ther road back, wen it cum thi 'ed t' dee,
An' thi tumbled on t't'desert sand, er fluttered dahn i't'sea?
An' which o' them swallas i' that sweepin' flock,
Wer 'atched i't'nest stuck under t'ledge, neer St. James's clock?

An' which 'appy brood o] fledglin's will it be that leaves,
T' fly sahth cum next autumntime, frae t'nest i't'vicarage eaves?
Then Harry upset mi wonderin', provin' Man's superior state,
Sayin, "T' swallas 'ev landed Brindle, but ther two er three days late!"

and went back to the Mobile Library. Yet even now, some 26 years later, I always look for that field full of marigolds at the corner of Broadfield in the warm May sunshine.

Much welcomed sunshine continued day after day as we rambled round the Lancashire countryside delighting in new sights and scenes on each route. Cottage gardens were ablaze with polyanthus, primulas, pansies, tulips, white rock, yellow alysum and my favourite, the mauve coloured aubretia. At School Lane in Brinscall, Mr. Barnes gave me some bedding plants and some good advice about the different types of soil which were best for each particular plant. His garden was a picture, with plants of all descriptions responding to his caring hands. Little Mrs. Rosemary Roberts of Dimple near Egerton gave me a root of comfrey (commonly known as knitbone because of its wonderful healing powers in repairing broken bones and joints). Some 25 years later, I still have this root which has now spread over my back garden and as I suffer from arthritis, I dry the leaves and bathe my swollen joints in an infusion of the leaves and stems. I also give a lot of these dried leaves to people suffering broken limbs. *"Its funny how these old remedies can still work wonders,"* I told Rosemary. She agreed and gave me two Feverfew plants, also known for their healing properties.

'Dimple' is a delightful name and consists of a few houses in the area just off the A666 road above Egerton which still have a wonderful view of the Belmont Moors and Winter Hill towering above all. How peaceful and quiet it was in those little country areas and rural villages at that time.

It's All Part of the Service.

One Thursday we were ambling along, visiting the farms on the road between Hawkshaw and Bradshaw enjoying the glorious sunshine and the beauty of the greening countryside. We were just turning up a farm track, when suddenly, a young woman whom I didn't recognise jumped out in front of the van gesticulating wildly and giving us a shock. Bill had to slam on the brakes and I heard a thud as 500 books cascaded onto the floor! I ignored them for the time being and opened the door. A pale young woman wearing tartan slacks and a red jumper which clashed with her red hair stood there.

"I'm so sorry to stop you, but please, I need help," she stuttered. *"My little boy's put his leg through the wooden floor of the barn and I can't get it out, it's stuck and it's swelling badly so I don't know what to do next. I've no phone, so I've just seen your van and wondered if you've any tools which could help ease the leg out?"* she finished breathlessly. *"Where's your house?"* asked Bill, *"and what's your name by the way?"* *"Oh, sorry. I'm Barbara Bent and my cottage is over there."* I looked at Bill as he knew about such things better than me. *"We'll come at once,"* he asserted, jumping from the van and locking it up.

We followed Mrs. Bent up the path where a small cottage and an old farmhouse appeared in the dip. Loud wailings were coming from the old barn at the side. We rushed in and sure enough, young David had got his leg stuck between the upper floorboards when they'd given way under his weight. I could see that the leg was already so swollen and badly bruised that any pulling or tugging would inflame it further still. Bill bent down and patted David's head. *"Don't cry son, we'll soon have you free,"* he soothed. *"If we can lever this piece of floorboard up from here then we can bring his leg up through the gap,"* said Bill. *"I'll go back for my toolkit and you can help Mrs. Bent,"* he told me. *"That leg looks awfully sore and swollen,"* I ventured. *"Have you tried putting some Vaseline round it or even margarine, as when it's more slippery, it's easier to move?"* Barbara Bent stared at me. *"No, no, as a matter of fact, I hadn't thought of that. I just pulled and pushed and David screamed with pain so I had to leave him and the leg started to swell making it harder than ever to move. I suppose I just panicked and ran out to look for help, as we've no immediate neighbours nor car nor phone,"* she finished. *"Go and bring some Bicarbonate of Soda dissolved in luke warm water and a piece of cloth. We'll bathe what we can see of the leg and help stop the bruising,"* I told her. *"Oh, and bring some Vaseline too!"* Mrs. Bent hurried indoors as I attempted to soothe 4 year old David. *"My leg hurts,"* he wailed. *"When's mummy coming back?"* At that moment Mrs. Bent appeared with all my requisites. She held David whilst I bathed the swollen leg carefully with the Bicarbonate of Soda solution, taking away the inflammation and soreness.

I was just attempting to smear Vaseline around the part where the leg met the jagged floorboard, when Bill arrived back with his toolbox. *"I've got a small saw and a chisel here,"* he stated, *"so we should be able to do something for the lad."* Mrs. Bent held David whilst I helped Bill. He inserted the chisel and levered up part of the cracked floorboard. Then, with the help of the saw and my hand on the chisel, he was able to saw round the edges and together, we lifted the offending piece of wood free, leaving David's foot dangling loose at last.

What a mess the leg was – badly swollen and black and blue. We didn't ask how he'd done it, but I continued to bathe the lower part of the leg which I hadn't been able to reach before in a bid to abate any further swelling. Mrs. Bent was in tears. *"How kind you are,"* she sobbed. *"I could have been here until my husband came home if you hadn't helped."* *"I really think you should let a doctor look at that leg. I couldn't see any splinters in it, but it's best to make sure,"* I said gently. *"But we've no car,"* she stated simply. I looked at Bill. *"Would you like us to run you to the doctor's surgery at Harwood or Bradshaw?"* I asked. *"Oh, would you? You're so kind,"* said Mrs. Bent. She locked the cottage. Bill wrapped David in a rug and carried him back to our van. *"The doctor can probably get an ambulance to bring you back,"* said Bill, *"as we have to finish our round and David may need to go to hospital."* Mrs. Bent held David tightly on the front seat as we approached Harwood. We stopped outside the surgery which was open all day, as there were nurses to attend to such incidents. *"Sure you don't want me to come in with you?"* I asked. *"No thanks, you carry on with your round and many thanks."* As we returned to our duties, I remarked to Bill that we weren't just a book service, but a community one as well.

Two weeks later, on the same farm track, a beaming Mrs. Bent met us with a lovely plant for me and a bottle of wine for Bill. Little David himself was with her, none the worse for his adventure, except for a bandage round his leg. *"The Bicarb' helped a lot to prevent further inflammation and bruising – they said so at the doctor's, Mrs. Moore,"* said Barbara. *"I'll remember that for the future."* We thanked her and said goodbye. *"Come and join the Mobile Library when you've time,"* I added.

A Deluge of Dogs.

Towards the end of the month we had a few days of rain, much to the relief of gardeners and allotment holders. It was on one of these wet sorties that we went to call on Mrs. Emma Crow, a lady whom I'd known in the 1960s when I was working on the Mobile Library, and whom I'd been delighted to see was still a member, although she'd changed her address. Emma now lived on a smallholding between Darwen and Turton and, as before, she bred dogs. Formerly, these had been dachshunds, but she'd now changed to Staffordshire bull terriers.

We arrived at Emma's smallholding and tooted the horn. She soon appeared, small and thin, her watery eyes made even more watery by the drips from her mackintosh, wrapped three times round her small figure. *"Gosh! I know this rain's needed, but my kitchen floor's filthy all the time, full of muddy paw marks. I'm sick of cleaning it."* In spite of her looks, Emma was friendly and kind and I enjoyed talking to her immensely. She had a sharp mind and was interested in anything and everything. She opened the library door to look out as she said she'd heard a noise, when suddenly she was knocked flying by a flood of Staffordshire bull terriers who trampled over her and swarmed into the Mobile Library. As she lay on the

floor, three of them went and stood on her and licked her lovingly and soggily round the face. There were at least twelve of them, and I was amused to see that some sported pink raincoats tied over their backs and fastened underneath by tapes. One or two had some pink plastic or vinyl babies' shoes over their paws. *"What the heck?"* Emma pushed off the offending dogs and struggled to her feet. She looked outside and saw the door of the dog's hut was swinging wide and that another four or five beasts were revelling in the mud and dancing round with their pink vinyl shoes, baying and barking vociferously. *"Who the hell's opened that door? I know I left it shut!"* Emma was livid.

The culprit, a boy of about 10 years appeared. *"Sorry Mrs. Crow, but mother sent the dogs some bones, and as you weren't around, I thought I'd throw them to them myself, then they all sort of got out and ran over me!"* I looked at the boy and burst out laughing. He was covered in slutch (as we call it in Lancashire) and two pink vinyl dog shoes were stuck on his pants. I thought Emma was going to explode, but both she and the lad looked so funny, she began to look a bit better. *"Help me round them up Alan and can you wait a minute please Mrs. Moore, then I'll get some hot water for the van floor."* The dogs didn't want to leave the van. They danced round the floor making it, their owner and Alan muddier than ever. The pink shoes and raincoats flew in all directions and I decided I'd better help as time was getting on. One huge animal evaded my arms and took a flying leap into the cab, landing almost on top of Bill who'd so far kept clear of the uproar. *"Jasper, come here AT ONCE!"* bellowed Emma, the stentorian voice belying her size. But Jasper licked Bill's face and snuggled against him, much to Bill's disgust. *"I'm so sorry,"* gasped Emma. *"They're real softies at heart you know."*

At length, order and sanity were restored and Emma returned with a mop, bucket, two mugs of coffee and scones to appease us. I thought it was funny and told Emma so as she mopped the muddy floor. *"Good job you have a sense of humour then,"* she added, as she extricated a pink shoe from under the section marked 'Religion'. *"Why the raincoats and shoes on some of them?"* I asked. *"Well, they are special dogs,"* said Emma. *"I'm showing them tomorrow and I want to keep their coats and paws as free from mud as possible, then they'll be easier to prepare for the show. This damned rain has just come at the wrong time for me."* I apologised for my laughter, but Emma said she didn't really mind as long as I didn't mind about the dirty floor. I thanked Emma for the coffee and scones and wished her luck for the show.

The rest of May was back to being warm and sunny. The hillsides were a picture of fresh green grass with young lambs, and streams leaping down over new growths of fern and moss. Up at Hollinshead Terrace in Tockholes after dinner one day, I walked a short way down Roddlesworth Woods and saw to my joy a haze of hyacinth and pale lavender. The wood was alive with bluebells. I could smell them long before I could see them and I thanked the Lord for His precious gifts of wild flowers and human senses of sight and smell. I drank my fill of the glory of the bluebells and walked back up the path. Leaning on the railings at the top, almost opposite the Royal Arms, I could see in the distance the mill at Abbey

Village, the unusual steeple of St. Paul's Church, Withnell, and Dole Lane winding round from the A675.

Time was getting on and the readers were waiting for us at the end of Hollinshead Terrace, all with their piles of books in their arms, or stored away in oil cloth and string bags which the older readers seemed to favour. Our 'special readers' at this stop were Gladys Taylor and her mother, Mrs. Ellen Brown. They were special to us because they filled our teapots with hot water for a 'brew' or for dinner, depending on which route or 'van run' we were on. We got to know them well and I often took Penny and Heidi to see the couple. 'Grandma Brown' was almost 90 years old, yet as sprightly as her daughter who was crippled with arthritis, so they had to look after each other. They were a wonderful couple and an example of selflessness and good living to all of us.

The solid stone houses on Bolton Road, Abbey Village, seen in March 1995. This is where Lily Marsden's toffee shop used to be.

TURTON TURNS UP TRUMPS: A JUBILEE DAY

The morning of June 7th dawned misty and warm. *"A sure sign of heat to come,"* my readers had told me many times. Sure enough, as I drove to Ramsbottom, the mist lifted above Holcombe Hill and the sky turned bright blue, with dazzling sunlight striking the whitewashed farms and cottages along Holcombe Road. Peel Tower beckoned me in the distance and as I swung round Ewood Bridge and up towards Edenfield, the whole majesty of that lovely hill assailed me, making me catch my breath at the sheer green beauty of my dear Lancashire. By the time I'd clambered into the Library van and we were heading towards Holcombe Brook, I could see that it was going to be a really beautiful summer's day. I was glad that we were going to some of the loveliest parts of our routes for scenery – Entwistle, Edgworth and Turton. I reflected how lucky I was to be actually paid for work which I loved so much. What a contrast this was with the dark satanic mill image that so many people have of Lancashire!

We coasted on through Hawkshaw, passing Croich Hey Old People's Hostel surrounded by lime trees. Turning right at the Bulls Head, I saw the spires of Edgworth Methodist Church and St. Anne's Church at Turton rising from the villages and I knew the reservoirs of Wayoh and Entwistle were just beyond. I'd always loved this view, and today it looked particularly lovely, the sun shining on it. We had two different days when we visited Edgworth and today it was the turn of the lower parts towards Turton Bottoms. Later we drove back towards Edgworth Post Office.

Our first stop was by the Barlow Institute, and a crowd of pensioners jostled for first place in the van. *"Morning Mrs. Moore."* Henry Boyson, as usual, mounted the steps first and blew his peppermint breath over me as he banged the books on the table. *"Bowling match today with Bromley Cross,"* he informed me, leafing through the latest 'Cowboy'. I listened with amusement as the old cronies argued about the pros and cons of how to get the best advantage. Little Mrs. Topping told me *"There's a pageant on in the grounds of St. Anne's Church this afternoon to celebrate the Diamond Jubilee of the school, I'm glad it's a lovely day for it."* *"What time does it start? I'd like to have a peep,"* I asked her. *"2pm,"* she said, *"but it won't be all that long. I believe all the village schools are taking part, so it should be very good."* As we were due in Turton later, I resolved to make time to have a look.

At the pleasant Post Office in Turton Bottoms, little Mrs. Mills came out and gave me some fresh bunches of mint with a special recipe for 'Edgworth mint sauce'. I thanked her sincerely, but as my culinary prowess is rather limited to more mundane dishes, I doubted if my sauce would be anywhere near as good as it should be! After the Post Office stop, we turned around and went up past Edgworth Post Office and towards Crown Point where several readers were discussing the pageant and their children's part in it. They urged me to take a look in if I could – even if it was only for 15 minutes. We turned left into Hob Lane; a little lane I'd always adored. Today, in the June sunshine, it was even more lovely than usual, with stitchwort, germander speedwell, harebells and bluebells all embroidering the roadside.

As always, I could not resist stopping on the causeway across the Wayoh Reservoir to look at and admire the beech and fir trees. We could also see the spire of Edgworth Methodist Church. Behind the pub in Edgworth village you could walk across the dam and see the water gushing from the overflow when in full spate.

Across the causeway we went, up past Holly Bank and Entwistle Hall – charming old buildings where the swallows wheeled and dived. On we went past Entwistle Railway Station and came to rest on the car park of that famous country pub, The Strawbury Duck. Edge Lane by the side of it was too narrow for our library van and so our readers from the farms up there came to meet us by the pub. They were all lovely people – all except one lady farmer that is. She was nice too, but she had a very bad habit – thus! We allowed a half an hour at this stop for readers to choose their books – plenty of time for most of them, but not this lady. Oh, she came to the van on time, alright, but never could decide just what she wanted to read! She'd career round the van with an armful of books asking me for suggestions and then completely ignored my choice! As the time drew near for our departure, I'd look at the clock and give subtle hints to her, but all to no avail. She'd pile her books on my table, then go and choose 6 or 7 more. *"I can't make up my mind today,"* she would say on every visit. Not only that, she'd also keep up a barrage of questions which I found quite wearing! In the end, I'd just say firmly; *"Sorry, we really must go now,"* and she would bang down the books in a huff, making sure she grabbed 3 more whilst I was charging (i.e. taking out the tickets) from her others. I had to grin and bear it.

Kind Mrs. Wallace from Railway Terrace (now Overshores Road) called for me to go and look at a robin's nest in her post box – right by her porch! I was thrilled to see the beautifully prepared nest when she tilted the postbox lid up, (the babies had gone by then). She said that the little bird had shown no fear of her or her family passing in and out so long as they didn't lock the door. As I turned round, there they were in the rowan tree in her garden, the mother robin and three babies with chests, not red but all speckly and cream as young ones are. I thanked Mrs. Wallace and we drove (very carefully I may add as the road was, and still is to this day, unmade) down to the Entwistle Reservoir and our last stop before dinner at the Water Bailiff's bungalow. Harry Jolley is a lucky man; fancy having

Harry, the Entwistle Reservoir water bailiff - Jolley by name and by nature.

a bungalow right on the side of the Entwistle Reservoir! The house went with the job. As I chatted to his wife, a jay alighted on the bird table in Harry's garden and he told me that it was a regular visitor, as was a greater spotted woodpecker.

What a gorgeous day this had turned out to be after all the mixed weather of the last few days. I'd never seen Entwistle Reservoir look more lovely and decided to walk all round it in my dinner hour, something I'd never done before. Bill drove to the other end to wait for me and had his dinner there, whilst I took my sandwiches and strode along the path round the water. Oh, I'm so glad I did, it was so quiet and peaceful. The combined beauty of the fir trees, the heady scent of bluebells and foxgloves like tall sentinels and the sunlight rippling the fresh, green beech leaves quite took my breath away. *"No foreign lake could be better than this today,"* I told myself. A tiny coal tit begged for crumbs from the lowest branch of a pine tree where she flitted when I sat down to eat. Two perky goldfinches gave me a cautious welcome from the safety of an alder tree and the sun sparkled and danced on the blue water. The woods were a haze of bluebells whose perfume filled the air and made it Paradise. How I enjoyed that walk! There was so much to see and hear. Tiny wrens warbled and a dipper by the water's edge bobbed to me. Foxgloves, tall and splendid like brave soldiers saluted me as I watched the busy bees eagerly climbing into the foxglove bells and doing the work that Nature intended for them.

I came back to the Mobile Library where Bill was snoozing in the sunshine. *"Come on,"* I told him, *"back to work, we've got a job to do."* Up Batridge Road we went and out onto Greens Arms Road which connects with the road between Bolton and Darwen at the eastern end. I was so happy I could hardly speak, back here in my own dear native countryside. One or two new houses had been built further down towards Turton village and we had a customer at one, a Mrs. Zanthie Rogers. I was intrigued with her name the first time I heard it, expecting to see a flowery lady in a big hat. But no, she was very down to earth with a cigarette hanging from her lips whilst she talked, and dyed blonde hair. *"My name? Well, mother read those very romantic novels you know and I think it came from one of them,"* she replied to my enquiry. Fascinated, I waited for her to flump up the path to her mansion in her blue felt slippers. *"She must have married into the aristocracy to get a house like that,"* I told Bill. However, on this day she turned up trumps by bringing out two glasses of lemonade which her housekeeper had made, and very good it was too. *"We've some unusual people, haven't we,"* I said to Bill.

In the village of Turton itself (or Chapeltown as some people call it) our visitors were fewer than usual, as most of them were helping at the pageant down at the church. We served what readers we could and cruised down to St. Anne's Parish Church. What a magnificent church it is too, with a most impressive spire which can be seen for miles around. The sun blazed down on the stalls that were out on the lawn. Bill sensed my longing. *"Go and have a quick look round, I'll wait here for you. We probably won't get many more customers now, they're too busy today and we've only Chapeltown Road to do before we finish."* I blessed him for his kindness and went into the church grounds. Sure enough, many of my readers were there and they smiled and made room for me on the rows of chairs. The children were all dressed in Edwardian clothes and the mothers in Victorian ones – some of the costumes were very authentic and I praised the mothers who'd concocted them.

The pageant began promptly at 2pm and I watched for a while, but then moved to browse around the numerous stalls which were manned by PTA members. Home made jam, chutney, pickles, fresh green produce, parkin and currant cakes all tempted me to buy and support a good cause. Three local schools were taking part, but it was actually St. John's Jubilee and someone told me that in 1991 St. Anne's Church would itself be celebrating 150 years of worship. I was pleased to see Mrs. Enid Barr there, a teacher at Hob Lane School for many years and much respected by all of Edgworth.

I felt a touch on my shoulder – I turned and a cup of tea was pressed into my hand. *"Come and have a sandwich and some strawberries and cream, I know you have to go soon."* Mrs. Lord was one of my readers from Chapeltown Road. *"Thank you, I will,"* I said and sat down at the table indicated where almost at once lots of home-made goodies were put in front of me. I would have liked to have watched more of the pageant, but duty called and Bill was patiently waiting down the road. I gave a donation for the PTA funds and reluctantly went on my way back to work. We completed our run in record time as most of our readers were up at the church. The sun still shone brilliantly on St. Anne's churchyard as we headed for Ramsbottom and home.

What a marvellous day I'd had – all that lovely scenery and then a bit of village life as well. *"I'll remember this day for years to come,"* I told myself. Twenty five years later, I still do, partly aided by the notes I made in my nature notebook and diary.

TO BONNY BELTHORN – TWO SHOULDERS OF MUTTON IN ONE DAY

I still can't decide which season I like best – Spring or Autumn. Is it Spring, when the gardens are teeming with brightly coloured flowers and everything seems fresh and new? Or is it Autumn, when the moors are ablaze with bell heather and ling and the road between Belmont and Abbey Village is bronzed with golden bracken and the trees reach their perfection of ochre and crimsoned flame? I don't think I'll ever be able to decide on one or the other. My eyes and heart are appreciative of both and the beauty that they give to our humble earth.

It was one lovely day in March when we set off along Bolton Road, Ramsbottom, for our visit to "Bonny Belthorn", some four miles from Accrington and about the same from Blackburn. Before we arrived, we had several calls to make. We turned right at the Hare and Hounds pub at Holcombe Brook onto the road leading to Holcombe Village, where we made a stop, by the Shoulder of Mutton Inn and Emmanuel Church, the Parish Church of Holcombe. Several villagers entered the van, cheerfully commenting on the warmth of the day and expressing thanks that the 'evil March wind' had subsided - at least for the time being.

Mrs. Little (who was very aptly named) imparted to us the information that her old tortoiseshell cat was behaving 'strangely' and could we find a book which would offer a suitable explanation? I looked at the cat books and also the ones on animal behaviour but nothing gave the symptoms that this weird 'moggy' seemed to have. *"Take her to the vet,"* said Vera Brown. *"Not I!"* retorted Mrs. Little, whose beady eyes missed nothing. *"He'll charge me a bomb and she's not worth it at eighteen years old."* *"Must be her age then,"* said George Benson. *"What's she doing, anyway?"* Mrs. Little looked suitably embarrassed. *"She keeps wee-ing on the doorstep in front of everybody and fancying the cocker spaniel next door. She's never done anything like this before and the cocker spaniel won't come out when she's around, so I'm not very popular round West Terrace,"* she finished, mournfully. *"Maybe she's suffering from distemper,"* said another bright spark. *"My husband suffers from that as well,"* said Brenda Booth. *"I give him Bob Martin's powder in his tea, two or three times a month and that seems to calm him down. Give your cat a dose, Mrs. Little, and it might do her some good."*

Past the pleasant little Holcombe school we went, and I looked down to the right towards contented Ramsbottom and Stubbins, glowing in the March sunshine. The green fields of Edenfield thrilled me as always, and the fields that we were

41

passing by the roadside were now gemmed with blush-tipped daisies and speedwells. The sky was a brilliant hyacinth blue, with tiny clouds like fluffy lambs drifting across it. I sighed with contentment as we ambled along. No need to rush on this route, I reflected. We'd plenty to do, but plenty of time to enjoy what we were doing. We came to Pleasant View Farm, where kind Mrs. Edmundson made us a welcome cup of tea, as she was always willing to do. Several new lambs, born in February were frisking around the fields nearby and I wondered how the twin black lambs at Woodnook Farm were faring.

Further along we had a stop at two bungalows where both families wanted books. Mrs. Isobel Jefferson was one of our readers there. She must have moved later to Helmshore, because when I began to write books and give talks, I met her again at the Musbury Friendship Club. Anyway, down the dip we went towards Helmshore - what a lovely little place it is - I could see the spire of St. Thomas' Church, Musbury, with the clock measuring the passage of time. We had just two stops to make near Helmshore Road, and then we moved on, past the Helmshore Textile Museum and towards the Holden Arms and Haslingden Cemetery. We turned left onto Grane Road, which always caught the bad weather. If there is any snow at all, Grane Road is always the first to suffer. Today, however, the green of the Grane and the glint of rainbows on the reservoirs was a sight not to be missed. St. Stephen's Church on the left, had been moved down the road from its original position to the place where it now stood. It had been pulled down stone by stone, each stone being numbered, so that when it was rebuilt, everything could be put back into the correct position, so Mr. Gardner, of the Holden Arms had once told me.

Along Grane Road we meandered, enjoying the spring sunshine, which made everything so much more pleasant. The gardens of some of the cottages were a splash of colour, with polyanthus, pansies and late crocuses, not to mention the deep raspberry of the flowering currant. I waved to Tom and Dick Taylor, the two old farmer brothers, famous for their dry stone-walling, who sometimes flagged us down to ask for books. but today our services were not needed. That stalwart old pub, the Grey Mare, hove into view and the landlady, Mrs. Forster, chose her books with great caution. *"Don't want any of them there 'rude' books upsetting my Ernie,"* she would say. What she did not know was that whilst I was attending to her needs, Bill would excuse himself, go to the pub toilet and slip Ernie a few sizzling novels to keep him happy for a couple more weeks anyway! *"I'm sure you're right Mrs. Forster, Ernie doesn't want any sexy books to upset him at his age, does he?"* I agreed. I would smile to myself as Bill climbed back into the driver's seat and winked at me.

The Congregational Chapel

Leaving the Grey Mare behind, we turned left and headed for Pickup Bank, a little hamlet on the moors above Hoddlesden and Darwen. We reached the right hand fork in the road and dipped down towards the cluster of cottages near Pickup Bank Old Chapel. This little chapel was, and still is, unique in that it has no services

The Grey Mare has stood on Grane Road at the junction with the road to Edgworth and Pickup Bank for many a year.

such as gas, water, electricity or sewage and is maintained entirely by a dedicated band of workers whose ancestors were trustees of the old building for many years. Built in 1835, Pickup Bank Old Chapel has outlived the new one which was built at Hoddlesden in 1900, and has since been pulled down. Three services each year are held in it. The character of the old Chapel is wonderful! There is an open fire and the floor is composed of bare flagstones, Tilley lamps and candles are used for lighting and the whole effect is quite spectacular at Christmas time when the Chapel is decorated with evergreens and holly.

On this day in 1972, we trundled down the track, past the old cottages and the chapel, down towards Old Rosin's Inn, a favourite country pub. We had one stop at two cottages on the way down, but the majority of our readers met us at Old Rosin's and chose their books there. As we drove on to the car park, several Land-Rovers were parked there with their drivers waiting to greet us. Many of the readers there were farmers or people who lived at outlying cottages or small-holdings, which we could not reach, so they came to us instead. There were a lot fewer modern distractions in those days, so our issues were very good, ranging from six to seven hundred on a busy day and three to four hundred on a quieter one. These farmers and farmers' wives certainly enjoyed their books. *"Morning Mrs. Moore,"* they all nodded or spoke to me as they mounted the van steps in big wellington boots and trilby hats or flat caps, and deposited their piles of books on the table. *"Morning,"* I replied, cheerfully discharging books and listening with delight to the broad Lancashire accents. *"Did you know Mrs. Walsh has had another baby boy?"* Mrs. Lowe asked me. *"That makes six now. I think she's trying for a football team,"* she continued, not giving me a chance to reply. *"More like her husband wants cheap labour on his farm,"* said Joe Hawkins, cheekily. I listened to the comments about bad backs; sciatica; the merits of Fennings Fever Cure; lumbago and all the general aches and pains that my elderly readers suffered from – all this in spite of the lovely day!

Not Many o' these in a Peawnd

"Where's Bob Eagles today?" I asked his neighbour. *"Should be coming,"* Joe Hawkins replied. *"He's not ill again, is he?"* I asked, concerned because Bob was an eccentric old recluse and not very reliable, either to look after himself or anything belonging to him, including his menagerie of dogs, cats, mice, rabbits, goats and hens. I remembered the time a few months ago, when I'd had to go to his smallholding because he had two books which had been on request for a month and he hadn't returned them. It was obvious that he wasn't coming to the van that day, so, leaving Bill in charge, I set off up the road towards Bob's house. The house was really more like a shack and was so dilapidated that it hardly looked fit to house a cow, never mind an old man. I knocked on the splintered door. *"Cum in."* The voice was deep and throaty. What a shock I got when I opened the door. A flagged floor, covered with sand and one or two old pegged rugs were the first things I saw. Then, in the centre of the room, a rickety old wooden table, on which were pieces of old newspaper, stuck down by jam - a jar of which was firmly entrenched next to an uncut white loaf and a bread-knife. As I stood there gaping, several brown hens scurried around the room and some, in their fright, flew either on to the table itself or on to the top of the mirror on the ancient dresser, which adorned the back wall. Bob himself was sitting in front of the oven and boiler range, with one of the doors open and his right arm pushed inside, presumably to keep warm. He wore one red and one blue wellington and a dirty, greasy flat cap on his head, and was obviously surprised to see me there. *"Aren't you well, Bob?"* The question was silly, really, because his red nose and flushed cheeks told me all I needed to know. *"What's tha cum here fer?"* he asked me. *"Sorry to bother you, but we need two of the books that you have. They were reserved for you and now they've been reserved for another reader, so I must get them back today,"* I told him. Bob rolled his eyes and indicated the pile of books I'd already noticed on the dresser. *"Them's theer if tha wants 'em, lass, but don't leave mi wi nowt to read till I can cum to yon van again."* *"O.K. Bob, I'll only take the two I need for now. You'll be fit enough to come to the van in a fortnight, I hope."* Bob was lighting his pipe with a piece of screwed-up newspaper, and was having great difficulty doing this. *"Why don't you use a match?"* I asked. *"Matches! Them's a shilling a box, an' I'm nod payin' that,"* said Bob. *"Paper's allus bin good enough fer me!"* he reiterated. *"Would you like me to make you a mug of tea whilst I'm here?"* I asked, feeling sorry for the old man. *"No thanks luv, I can manage a bit yet. Mi sister'll be cumin' later on."* I wondered what Bob's sister thought about her brother's living quarters and the way he lived, but that was none of my business. The hens

had apparently decided I was no threat to them and were now on the table attacking the bread and jam. Several had also flown onto the rack up above the fire, where Bob's underpants and combinations dangled embarrassingly in front of me, and they made flying sorties onto the dresser narrowly missing two old pot dogs which adorned it. It was like something from the last century and I wish that I'd taken a picture of it all, but I hadn't my camera with me at the time. *"I hope you'll soon be better Bob,"* I said as I picked out the required books. *"Maybe we'll see you in two weeks time, eh?"* For an answer Bob gave a HUGE blow into his handkerchief and nodded to me.

Back at the van, Bill had listened in astonishment to my description of Bob's living quarters. Still, we'd had old recluses before, I reflected - like Tommy Riley from the Withnell area, who had died recently. They all seemed to manage remarkably well too! To me, it was all a matter of interest and concern about my readers, and I never failed to be amazed at the adventures we had, the tales they told, nor the scenes we witnessed as we serviced their reading needs.

Joe Hawkins had been right. I glanced through the van door and saw Bob Eagles bumping down the track in his dilapidated truck. True to form, his old wellingtons on his feet, his books encased in an old oilcloth bag. *"Just remembered it wer yer day,"* he remarked. *"Asta getten owt on pigs, lass? I'm thinkin' o' rearin' two fer bacon, like."* I looked round the shelves. *"Try this for now and I'll bring some more next time,"* I promised, and handed over a general farming book. *"Thanks, lass."* Bob's wizened cheeks were ruddy and perspiring. *"Reckon spring's on t' way,"* he remarked, as he lumbered round the van, his wellingtons flapping round his legs. *"Aye, it's time tha got them woollen combinations off, Bob,"* said Joe Hawkins. *"I reckon they're causin' a smell round here,"* he added, wickedly. Bob blushed slightly and I felt sorry for him. *"It's easy to see ther's no woman teks care o' thee Bob."* Jim Talbot, another doughty old farmer, was enjoying the fun. *"Don't need a woman,"* said Bob. *"I 'as mi hens to keep mi company, and THEY don't answer back,"* he said, ominously. *"Then tha'll not be hen-pecked, like Joe then,"* said Jim and whisked out of the van before anyone could say anything else. *"We do have fun, don't we?"* said Bill, as the old farmers and farmers' wives retreated in a cloud of smoke from their ancient Land-Rovers.

Another Gem – Owd Jem.

Another old character at Pickup-Bank was 'Jem o' Rosins' (real name James Townsend). A marvellous old man who'd been the first child to be christened at the new chapel, built in Hoddlesden in 1900. He never actually came to the van for books, but we sent books for him via his daughter, Mrs. Marion Rollinson, who is still one of the stalwarts at the Pickup Bank Chapel. There were many, many characters living in and around the Pickup Bank area and we were privileged to have some of them as our readers. I enjoyed my meetings with them very much and knew that on every visit we'd be in for a drama of some sort.

Back towards the Grey Mare we bounced, along the narrow winding road, with rough moorland on each side, then we turned left and headed for Belthorn.

This was, and still is, a community where everybody seemed to be related by either blood or marriage. High on the moors above Blackburn and Oswaldtwistle, Belthorn has the dubious distinction of having some parts of the village in Blackburn and others in what was then the Oswaldtwistle U.D.C area. Much was made of this great divide. The Blackburnians considered themselves superior because they had bigger dustbins and dustcarts, so Mrs. Lee once informed me. However, the 'Ossie-ites', as they were nicknamed, claimed that Oswaldtwistle was a much nicer and homelier little town than big brother Blackburn. and pointed to the moors and surrounding hills with lovely panoramic views 'on our side!' Yet, it seemed that no matter that a boundary divided them, they were united in the defence of their own little community and were fiercely protective of their own village culture and speech. This I found out to my cost on one visit, when I mildly suggested that one Janie Bond should change the name of her cottage from "Down th'en ole" to something a shade nicer. Little Lizzie Flegg attacked me like a fighting cock with spurs at the ready and her neck pushed forward, red with rage.

"Thee mind thi own business young woman. Tha knows nowt about yon cottage - it wer her granny's, as kept hens ther fer fifty years, an hoo doesn't want owt changin'." As the cottage looked like it hadn't seen a lick of paint for centuries, and Janie herself still dressed in Victorian clothes, I knew what she meant. I blushed and murmured a brief apology, which was accepted with a curt nod. Then, suitably chastened, I attended to my duties and vowed to be more careful in future.

On this particular day, our first stop in Belthorn was at Tower View, a row of houses facing Darwen Tower, which blazed defiantly in the March sunshine, stoically defending the old town of Darwen in the valley below. *"Morning Mrs. Moore. Morning, morning."* The greetings were cheerful and sincerely dispensed as piles of library books were put onto my table. After my readers at this stop had satisfied their needs we rumbled down Belthorn Road past the rows of cottages whose gardens only sported the hardier shrubs such as daphne and forsythia, because of the cold winds which bedevilled the village. *"Very cold but healthy living up here,"* said Tom Grimes, and certainly his ruddy complexion bore out his observation.

The Dog Inn was a focal point for all the villagers, and one of our busiest stops. It was good to listen to these hard-working people, their philosophy of life was simple and practical: Work hard, spend carefully, be a good Christian and enjoy your food and drink. It certainly seemed to have stood them in good stead, as most of them lived to a ripe old age! Miss Tilly Martin, an eccentric but gentle lady, who had previously had her books exchanged by one of her neighbours, but who now came to the van herself, appeared at the door, her black cloak around her shoulders. *"Mrs. Moore, can you find me something on goats? I'm thinking of keeping a few they are so VERY affectionate,"* she burbled. I grinned as I searched the shelves, visualising Miss Tilly with the goats sitting down at the table with her, whilst she ate! It was just the sort of thing she would encourage, I decided, as I handed her a copy of 'Goat Husbandry'.

46

Nancy with the Laughing Face.

One of my favourite readers, further down Belthorn Road, was Mrs. Nancy Gabbott of Prospect Terrace, which was round the back of Belthorn Road. She was about seventy years old at this time, and a wonderful example of a good-living woman. She would come into the van with her sister, Miss Eccles, and another lady, Mary-Alice Bury. They would really enjoy looking round the shelves and were very appreciative of the books we had on offer. Nancy would take our teapot to brew the tea for us and, as she left the van she would whisper to me, discreetly, *"If tha wants to use t'closet lass, cum round later when you cum fer t' teapot."* (I usually took advantage of her offer as soon as I could). With her floral apron, or 'brat' - as we used to call it, and her headscarf round her curly grey hair, Nancy epitomised that generation of Lancashire women who had devoted a lifetime to working in the cotton mills and bringing up the family at the same time - a task they performed with great care and dexterity, at no small sacrifice to themselves! I used to slip round to Prospect Terrace to collect the teapot and, in winter, I was glad of the warm fire in Nancy's spotless house. I remained friends with Nancy and her daughter, Vera, when I had left the Mobile Library and they had moved to a lovely little cottage on Belthorn Road itself.

This mad March morning, however, I first ran up to the Belthorn Post Office on Holden Street to post a letter. Further up on Chapel Street stood the old Belthorn Chapel. Many of the villagers had been christened there and had attended Sunday School and Chapel services, all their lives. I stood and looked at the imposing old building and wondered how many families had worshipped there over the years. In the long hot summer of 1995, I called at the Post Office again for a paper, then walked up to where the chapel had once stood - it had been demolished some years before - and was surprised to see a number of common orchids flourishing in the graveyard and where the building itself had stood. Was the soil full of chemicals? I wondered, as orchids usually flourish where the soil is acidic or has deposits of chemicals in it.

Walking back to the van, I noticed several of the village ladies were out, mopping their doorsteps and flags and then donkey-stoning them afterwards. This was an old Lancashire custom which was still very prevalent in the early 1970s. Donkey-stones were usually given by the 'Rag and Bone' man, who travelled the back streets. On this particular March day, I watched this old ritual being performed with great pride and care. The elderly ladies were on their knees, mopping, scrubbing, drying with a clean cloth and, finally, applying the donkey stone to the doorstep with as much flourish as an artist painting a picture, and they vied with each other to produce the fanciest pattern. Much cheered by their devotion to duty and Lancashire pride, I smiled and wished them 'good morning' as I walked back to the van.

Two Angels in Paradise.

Down Belthorn Road we rumbled, leaving the village behind but still having one or two more cottages and farms to visit before we reached Guide. It was too

47

early for the swallows to have arrived but, all the same, I looked out for them at the old farm on the left, where I knew they nested. *"No sign of them yet,"* I told Bill. *"They're usually at this farm before anywhere else - it's mid-April before they get to Rising Bridge,"* I added for his benefit. We turned right at Guide traffic lights, into School Lane and along to a building called 'Paradise Cottage', wherein dwelt two dear old ladies with the quaint names of Prudence Heaven and Patience Bliss. How I marvelled at these two old friends and the simple way that they lived. I usually took some books to the cottage for them, as they had great difficulty in climbing the steps, so I knew what the inside of the cottage looked like. The first time I saw it I was amazed, for the front room walls were covered with religious texts of every shape and size. *"Have faith, all ye who enter here,"* a large framed embroidered text urged me as I entered the door. *"He is Lord!"* proclaimed a cross-stitched bookmark, hanging on the budgie's cage. *"The wrath of the Lord be upon you,"* glared at me from above the fireplace, and many, many more beautifully embroidered pictures, tapestries, cross-stitched texts, knitted and crocheted samplers and squares, all bearing a divine message for sinners, such as me, to read, mark and learn. A huge crucifix hung in front of the mirror, pressed flower tablemats, with suitably chastening thoughts, adorned the parlour table and even the chair-back covers urged me to *"Repent, repent ye sinner man".* Once I'd got over the initial shock, I looked forward to my fortnightly visit to these two 'saints', as I described them to Bill.

On this day, Miss Prudence herself, greeted me at the door, looking like an earthly angel with her pink face aglow and her floral dress floating round her like a hot-air balloon. *"Come in my dear. What have you brought for us today?"* she inquired, gently. She swept before me into her saintly parlour, where Miss Patience welcomed me and delicately sniffed into a lavender scented handkerchief. *"Praise the Lord, you've come to us again,"* she intoned, as she looked through the pile of books I'd taken. *"Prudence, I don't really think we should read 'Far From The Madding Crowd', do you?"* *"It's a good story,"* I assured that modest lady. *"Yes, but there may be parts of it that are HEATHEN and it could corrupt my mind,"* Miss Patience simpered, lowering her eyes to a text on a traycloth. *"You're quite right, dear! With a title like that, it could be about an asylum, in which case it would upset us, so I think we will leave that today, Mrs. Moore,"* said Prudence. *"What a job it is, choosing the right kind of books for these two saints,"* I thought, as I hastily removed a Catherine Cookson book from the pile and hid it until I went out! However, I eventually managed to satisfy them with a selection of light humour and country books and, as always, they were very appreciative and profuse with their thanks. The front parlour was decorated with daffodils and forsythia, enhancing the religious texts and needlework delicacies to their full advantage. The two old ladies, with their wispy grey hair, baby pink cheeks and cherubic expressions, exactly matched their names, I reflected. They certainly practised what they preached, as I'd never heard a wrong word about them and everyone said they were such good living creatures that they were sure they were saints, or angels, in human disguise. As they thanked me, I felt very humble as I reflected on

Nancy Gabbott of Belthorn Village, a regular library user, was 97 years old when this photograph was taken in 1994.

their modest way of living and the enlightening texts. Along Lottice Lane we swept towards the Britannia Inn and Mrs. Waite's bungalow on the corner. Mrs. Waite was the elder daughter of Mrs. Nancy Gabbott, of Belthorn, whom we had seen that morning. In the summer she and her husband, Bob, sold tomatoes, lettuces, carrots and other fresh vegetables for the benefit of non-growers, like me. The library routes had been altered recently and now we went to Belthorn in the morning and called at the houses and farms along the A677 in the afternoon, after visiting Mount St. James, Knuzden, and then ending up at Cross Edge and Green Haworth, all on the same day.

Owd Jim at t' Britann.

Old Jim Whewell, landlord of the Britannia Inn, was waiting for us, a pile of westerns in his arms. He often gave us a lemonade in summer, or a hot drink and a warm at his fire in winter, and was one of our most interesting readers, as he had many tales to tell. Today he was anxious for us to find him something on building hen-cotes, as his son, Bill, had started rearing hens. We had nothing specific on the subject so I made out a request slip, for the next visit. Then it was down to Greenfield Terrace and Duckworth Hall, where a variety of readers, old and young, awaited us. There used to be a mill there, and some of our readers had worked there for many years. They often told me tales of their working days spent in Duckworth Hall Mill. We had our dinner on the piece of spare ground opposite the Britannia Inn, where we had a good view of the crossroads.

After dinner, we turned round and drove towards Blackburn, calling at houses along Haslingden Old Road on the way. The hedgerows were full of sparkling celandines and, on pieces of waste ground, the sunny little coltsfoots smiled up at me. Garsden Avenue is a small cul-de-sac off Haslingden Old Road and we stayed at the top for the borrowers to come to us, as it was difficult turning the van round in such a small place. Ben Turner was our main customer here and he was very proud of the lettuces and vegetables that he grew in his back garden. He never failed to give Bill and me gardening advice, and today was no exception. *"Do you*

Jim Whewell, landlord of the Brittania Inn, Oswaldtwistle, for many years found time for reading. Tales of 'Owd Jim' are part of local folklore.

want sum 'orse-muck?" he asked, casting his eyes around the books marked 'Romance'. *"Best thing out fer yer garden if you dig it in now."* Now, although I love and can identify most garden and wild flowers, I am not really a good gardener, as I haven't much time to spare, so the idea of digging in a load of horse manure didn't really appeal to me. But Ben persisted in extolling the virtues of this tangy fertiliser. *"Let me bring you a dolly-tub of it,"* he enthused. *"You can get it home in the library van, then he can have some as well."* He nodded at Bill, who kept his eyes firmly on the book he was reading. I could see I'd have to handle the matter on my own this time! *"Well, you're very kind, Mr. Turner, but I couldn't possibly have a dolly tub here in the van when I'm serving customers."* Ben opened his mouth to protest, but I'd had an idea and I said, quickly: *"Why don't I bring my husband round one weekend, with his van, then, if he wants some, we can collect it then, thank you..."* I added. Ben seemed slightly mollified. *"Yes, that's okay, then I can tell him how to dig it in good and proper,"* he replied. I breathed a sigh of relief as Ben turned his attention to choosing more books and eventually left us in peace.

Kitty and Cat.

On we ventured to Mount St. James at Knuzden, where St. Oswald's Church beamed in the afternoon sunshine. Further up the road was the village of Stanhill, the birthplace of James Hargreaves, of 'Spinning Jenny' fame. We didn't serve the village as it was near enough to Oswaldtwistle library for the villagers to use that, but we did sometimes get requests from elderly readers there. We had about five readers at Knuzden. One of them was Kitty Bond, who always brought her tabby cat called 'Humbug' with her wherever she went in a closed wicker basket. Why on earth she needed to take him everywhere, I don't know, but neighbours had told me that she'd lost all her family through tragic circumstances, and Humbug was the only security she had left. As usual, the cat basket was deposited on my desk whilst Kitty chose her books, and I must say that the animal never made a sound, or a 'muff', as we say in North East Lancashire, so he must have felt quite contented in his cosy bed. I called his name through the basket and was rewarded by a deep purring sound from within. Humbug was alive and well, I surmised. Kitty offered me a sticky piece of homemade treacle toffee, which I accepted with glee. *"That'll keep thi trap shut fer a bit,"* pronounced Tom Woods, and as my teeth were stuck together, I couldn't even grin!

We turned back onto the A677, calling at Ye Olde Brown Cow Inn, which served delicious meals, Nook Lane Garage and Broughton Barn Cottage. We ambled up tracks to various farm houses and cottages, which looked down on the little town of Oswaldtwistle, drowsing below in the March sunshine. We passed the site of the old Cocker Brook Day School and Chapel, where some of our readers had attended and worshipped, years ago. Today, the landlord of The Coach and Horses didn't want to change his books, so we continued round the corner to Ramsclough Farm, where Mrs. Whitworth was feeding two lambs which had had difficulty in suckling from their mother. She called me into the kitchen to see them. *"This is*

Annabelle and Sophie." She indicated two tiny lambs, now stretched out on the old peg rug, in front of a roaring fire. I watched with interest as she held a feeding bottle in each hand, whilst the animals rose and eagerly nuzzled the teats. Kind Mrs. Whitworth guided the teats into their mouths and they soon got the hang of sucking the milk. *"These two were late arrivals and nearly died,"* Mrs. Whitworth told me. *"I've fed them for three days and I think they're going to be alright now,"* she ventured, as she left the lambs basking in the glow of the homely fire, to come and choose her library books.

There is a Green Hill.

Green Haworth Chapel was a landmark for miles around, and the cottages at Cross Edge had a wonderful view across the towns and valleys below. On clear days you could see not only Pendle Hill, but Ingleborough as well and, as this was just such a day I took out my binoculars, which I kept in the van, and had a good look at the greening countryside and the hills in the distance. Just below the cottages at Cross Edge and leading down to Fielding Lane were some more cottages called 'Newthorn', and further on still was Gaulkthorn Farm. One or two readers from Newthorn Cottages came to choose books from us up at Cross Edge, and one of these was eighty year old Annie Berry, who defied all the odds against rheumatism by climbing the steep little hill to reach our van, when it stopped outside the Shoulder of Mutton. *"Funny that we should start the day at one Shoulder of Mutton at Holcombe, then finish at this one in Oswaldtwistle,"* I remarked to Bill. Mrs. Gill, the landlady of the pub entered wearing her floral apron and headscarf tied in a turban round her head. *"I'm in the middle of spring-cleaning,"* she informed me, *"and Mrs. Bates is just giving the rugs a good beating. They certainly need it, with the mud we get up here when it rains,"* she continued. I looked to the left, where Mrs. Bates, her face red and contorted, was angrily banging the poor, hapless rugs, with an old-fashioned carpet-beater.

"Couldn't she just vacuum them?" I asked. *"Surely it would be easier all round."* Mrs. Gill looked affronted. *"My pub is always properly bottomed,"* she ventured. *"Not like some as I can mention, and that means beating the rugs and the carpets every March."* I thought of my own house, with the spring-cleaning not even started, and did not say another word. Mrs. Gill buzzed round the shelves, chose her books in record time and buzzed out again, back to her own little abode, which would soon be fit for the queen herself to visit.

Further along Cross Edge and towards Accrington, past the diminutive Green Haworth School, incorporating the church of St. Clement's, was the Red Lion pub, at the end of a row of cottages called 'Moorgate', but known colloquially as 'Bedlam'. We didn't serve these cottages, as they were in Accrington, but, if time permitted, I used to walk along and take a look at them, as the name fascinated me. I asked my readers about the origin of the name, but no-one seemed absolutely certain. One theory was that a man made sweets known has 'Bedlam Humbugs' in his little cottage there, and sold them all over the Willows Lane and Fern Gore area of Accrington. Afterwards, people called at the cottage for them. Another

The Dog Inn, Belthorn, stands on a hillside providing shelter against the elements for travellers and local residents.

reader said that, at one time, someone from the cottages would call themselves 'The Mayor of Bedlam' and would hold a tea-party to celebrate his induction. There seemed to be a rivalry between the 'Cross-Edgers' and the 'Bedlamites', and they each kept to their own territory - the 'Edgers' shopping in Oswaldtwistle and the 'mites' in Accrington. My readers at Cross Edge and its neighbours, were very circumspect about their reading and chose suitable titles with great care on every single visit.

Today, the sun was still shining and the pussy-willows fluffing as we said 'goodbye' to Cross Edge and made our way back along Broadfield, past Red Walls and Sandy Beds Farm, to the corner of the field where we again joined the A677. Our next stop, Mount Pleasant Farm, stood on the right, with magnificent views from the kitchen windows *"I could wash up there, myself,"* I told Bill, as Mrs Dean bustled out to exchange her books. *"Yes, it's lovely,"* she replied to my comments *"I hardly think I'm doing a chore when I look out of the kitchen window."* Mrs. Dean was a widow, but she had two fine strong sons, who ran the farm for her, and she baked and cleaned and washed for them, happy to be of service, in the home which had been in her husband's family for about two centuries. *"I must rush today, I've some spring-cleaning to do,"* she announced. *"Not another one,"* I thought, as we cruised back to Ramsbottom, past the Farmers Glory and down Roundhill Road and Hud Hey into Haslingden.

HALCYON DAYS – WITH WHINBERRIES FOR DESSERT

The days seemed to fly by as they always do when you're enjoying yourself so much and I certainly did enjoy my work on the Mobile Library. That year a warm May ambled into a rather cooler June, but it did not spoil the delights of the countryside for me. June, the month of roses, hollyhocks, giant sunflowers and blood red peonies which graced the gardens of my readers in their village homes. The hedges and hedgerows were embroidered by 'Queen Anne's Lace', red campion, hemp agrimony, meadow cranesbill, and other precious and brightly coloured tiny flowers, as well as the ubiquitous cow parsley. Threads of convolvulus, honeysuckle and briar roses entwined themselves round the hawthorn and ivy. The grass verges were ablaze with purple and yellow vetch, bird's foot trefoil, speedwell and stitchwort flowers.

Driving back from Hoddlesden one day via the Entwistle road and the Crown and Thistle, I looked across at the moor which was brilliantly purpled with bell heather and amethyst shades of ling. *"You could imagine you're in Scotland, it's so lovely here,"* I told Bill. Darwen Tower stood sentinel above the industrious old town stretched below in the valley, as if guarding and watching over its people, no doubt some of them ancestors of the men who'd built the tower itself, years before. The imposing chimney of India Mill was also a special landmark to the people of Darwen. Its fame and magnificence has been written about all over the world and Darwen inhabitants are justly proud of it. Most families in Darwen had had somebody working at the India Mill at some time or another and the closure of this old stalwart in early 1990 was a sad day for Darwen.

The end of June and the four weeks of July comprised the 'Wakes Weeks' holidays for my readers from Bolton, Bury, Turton, Accrington, Darwen and some Blackburn areas. The first to return their books and ask for extended loans for the next lot because they were going away were the people from Harwood, Bromley Cross and nearby villages. There were very few holidays spent abroad then and the most common places were Llandudno, Scarborough, Morecambe, Southport, the Lakes and Blackpool, although some older people now had cars and were becoming more adventurous by driving down to Devon and Cornwall. But my readers, bless their old-fashioned hearts, wanted 'no truck' with the hippy, swinging, jean-clad youth of the early 1970s, so most of them did what they'd done for years and caught the coach to the resort of their choice. I was included in the audience of their holiday adventures when they got back, and listened eagerly to their tales.

For Better or For Worse

George Newton was a grumpy old farmer who wouldn't go away and leave his livestock. So, in the end, his poor long-suffering wife went away for two weeks and left him to fend for himself. I didn't blame her either, the way he grumbled about everything. Daisy Newton was a real gem and often made us laugh about George and his 'humbug' ways. She came into the van one day, much refreshed after two weeks at Bridlington on her own. *"The old scrooge,"* she relayed *"he didn't feed the cats or the hens whilst I was away and I only just got back in time to stop most of them dying of starvation. He's a miserable cur,"* she continued, *"hates cats and hens and anything else that's weak and feeble. And you should have seen the kitchen when I got back – half full of dirty pots, pans, dirty washing. He'd not done a thing! Its a good job I've had a break,"* she added, *"although there was so much work when I got back, I wondered if it had been worthwhile my going away at all."* I hastily assured her that the rest and certainly the change would have done her good! Then George himself appeared on the scene yawning widely and showing ugly yellow teeth in a shrunken mouth. *"You finished yet?"* he bellowed at Daisy. *"Just coming my sweet."* She gave us a quick smile and went back to the lion's den. *"I don't know how she puts up with him,"* said Bill, and we thankfully shut the van door and went to our next port of call at the village of Affetside.

Jacob Joins In.

Our first stop was at 'Sugar Plum Cottage' inhabited by one Jacob Taylor who was badly crippled with rheumatism yet always managed to keep cheerful and smiling. He shuffled to the door, his badly swollen feet encased in comfortable felt slippers which accommodated his incapacity. He wore a black cap, black trousers and a waistcoat that was too small for him, but his brown eyes twinkled as I hastened to help him. *"Thanks love,"* he winced as he mounted the steps with great difficulty. *"Can you find me a book on breeding rabbits?"* he enquired. I duly obliged, as this was one of the duties I enjoyed most, helping people to find the books and information they wanted. If we hadn't got what they required at that time, then I'd make out a request slip for them and bring it back on the next visit. Jacob surprised me when he said suddenly *"I'm thinking of geddin' some of them theer jeans to go over mi combinations. I believe as they're very warm."* I looked at Jacob's bowed legs and smiled as I imagined him in blue jeans with a leather belt around his middle and a Stetson on his head. *"Dusta know owt about 'em, love?"* he added. Jeans were only just coming to be part of everyday life then and I certainly didn't wear them, so I didn't know much about them. *"If I were you, I'd go to a good Army and Navy Stores and get some good thick trousers, they'll be much better and warmer than jeans,"* I stated. Jacob's face fell. *"Do you really think so?"* *"Go into a shop and try a pair on, then you can see for yourself,"* I advised. (Personally, I thought that he was too old and bent and would look totally incongruous in jeans, but I hadn't the heart to say so) Anyway we left it at that and drove further up the road. Imagine my surprise then, when some three months later, Jacob appeared in the door in a pair of nice Wrangler Jeans and stout new boots – *"to help support mi poor feet,"* he ventured as I looked down at his legs bowed like an arch in a garden, a shade of brilliant blue. I wanted to laugh as my imagination ran riot and I saw Jacob as 'The John Wayne of Affetside' with a six-shooter and a Stetson to accompany his cowboy jeans. However, as he seemed to like them and they kept him warm and were practical (or so he said) I refrained from deriding them too much and kept my doubts and remarks for Bill later.

Two Angels in Clogs.

Further up Affetside, on Watling Street, lived two real old Lancashire sisters, Mary-Alice and Sarah-Alice (pronounced Seralice). That's one of the interesting things about old Lancastrians, their dialect and the way they pronounce and elongate particular vowels and words. Even towns which are only a few miles apart have their own distinctive dialect, and often unusual words as well. Mary-Alice and Seralice were very parochial indeed and had lived in the same cottage for over eighty years, only venturing into Bolton or Bury when it was absolutely necessary. In the early 1970s, there were still vans delivering fresh bread, meat and vegetables, so apart from an occasional sortie to the Co-op shops, they were quite happy to live at 'Thrushes' Nest'. I heard from other readers that Seralice had been a good singer in her time, like her mother before her.

Well, the first time I saw them, they were like something out of this world with huge, fierce looking steel curlers in their hair and purple hairnets vainly attempting to cover the hideous things. They still wore clogs and the old-fashioned Lancashire black wollen stockings. On that first encounter, now some 25 years ago, they eyed me suspiciously and whispered to each other that I was obviously *"...one o' them flighty young monkeys as weren't fit to serve decent people."* I was rather taken aback by this description of myself, but was assured by Bill that they'd get used to me and come round in time. I was always polite to them even if their clogs did make a tremendous din and they both kept clicking their false teeth much to my, and the other readers', annoyance! I knew I'd passed the test when Seralice asked me one day, *"Esta any o' them theer rum books? Tha knows, them wi' plenty o' reet good romance an' lovin' in 'em."* Seralice rolled her baleful eyes at me surreptitiously. I choked on a laugh. *"Why yes, of course Miss Bolton. Have a look at these,"* and I pushed several of that category of book in her hand. *"Thank you very much young woman, an' if tha' waits theer, I'll fetch thee an' 'im some currant cake wi best butter on id."* *"My,"* remarked Bill as Seralice clattered out of the van, *"You've made a hit there I think. First time we've been given anything off them two old sceptics,"* he finished. I grinned at his very apt description of these two ancient Lancashire Natives.

One warm day in July we cruised over towards Edgworth and Wayoh Reservoir visiting some farms there. The scenery was wonderful, and the hedges down Hob Lane were full of ragged robin, foxgloves, yellow toadflax and a myriad of tiny flowers which had replaced the primroses and bluebells. Oh, how I loved to be out and about like this. We later called back at 'Honey Hole' near Broadhead Road, the home of that sprightly spinster Miss Marigold Masham. She'd been out to Bolton when we'd called earlier, or so her neighbour told us. So, as we were 'up and down and roundabout' the various farm tracks and country lanes, we were passing near her cottage and this time she was in. *"How kind of you to call back,"* she twittered. *"I hate to miss my books, but I had a dentist's appointment in Bolton and it was the only time he could fit me in!"* I assured her, *"We are here at your service as much as we can be."* Miss Marigold, whose red hair flamed out behind her like a horse's long mane chose her books with care. *"Have you got any new Ruth Rendell's?"* she asked, *"or can you recommend a good historical novel, dear?"* Eventually she settled for six books all entirely different in subject matter, so I still don't know to this day who her favourite authors are. *"Just wait a moment,"* she said and took the books indoors. She returned five minutes later with coffee and two slices of delicious home-made whinberry pie and cream. *"These whinberries are scrumptious,"* I told her. *"Where did you get them from?"* *"Well, I went walking round Broadhead Road and Edgworth last week. There's some real beauties up there,"* she told me. I resolved to investigate all whinberry bushes up that area as soon as I got the chance. Meanwhile, on with the job!

Animal Hospital.

We trundled down the bumpy lane to 'Rookery Nook' where Mrs. Tabitha Snape lived in her gypsy caravan. She said she wasn't of any gypsy origin when I asked her, but she certainly looked like one with her long grey hair which had once been black, and dangling earrings to match her dazzling bracelets. She had started a kind of voluntary 'Wild Bird Hospital' when I'd first met her some years before. Later she was joined by her widowed friend Betty Clamp and together they ran not just a Wild Bird Sanctuary but a hospital for injured animals as well. These two kind-hearted ladies did a lot of good work, funded entirely by themselves and voluntary contributions from members of the public. They'd also quite a kind of 'miniature zoo' accumulated over the years composed of either unwanted of injured creatures, or those that they'd grown so fond of they couldn't bear to part with after they'd been treated and declared fit and well. On this particular day, there they were, squawking and flapping around Tabitha and Betty as we pulled onto the grass. 'Rookery Nook' still lived up to its original name, as there were four of the black horrors cawing and screeching over our heads as we talked. *"Come and look at my latest acquisition,"* Tabitha invited, and I was introduced to Charlotte, the baby pig whose mother had refused to suckle her. Tabitha patted the little pig's head and spoke gently to her. *"This is Mrs. Moore. Now offer a paw, Charlotte. Good pig, good girl,"* as a muddy paw was proffered and accepted by me. In an old tin bath behind the caravan lived Harry, the one legged frog, together with a strange assortment of injured newts, other frogs and toads. Poppy, the three-legged cat was basking blissfully amongst the calendulas watched nervously by Holly the doormouse and Pinky, the one-legged Chaffinch. Dolly the goat, who'd had most of her hair cruelly torn off her, was watching Snuffles the hedgehog and her two babies who'd all been hit by a car which didn't stop. One of the villagers who'd been behind the hit-and-run driver had rescued the injured hedgehogs and brought them to Tabitha and Betty, who'd nursed them and made pets of them. Later, I persuaded Tabitha to give me one of the baby hedgehogs to nurse and look after for the winter. 'Binky', as we called her, delighted Penny and Heidi for months afterwards by hibernating in our shed and then emerging into the garden in spring and allowing them to play with her. My husband, Gordon, built Binky a little hedgehog house of her own but she didn't produce any babies for quite some time.

Tabitha and Betty loved all their charges, great and small. An old tortoise called Terry, whose owners had thrown him out for dead, had been rescued and was now resting under the apple tree. Meanwhile, Margy the goose with a collar round her fractured neck, Millie the Mallard with a broken wing and Mandy the old white leghorn hen who'd had her comb and wings mauled by a dog were sharing a sprinkling of corn by the duck pond. *"They do you both credit,"* I told Tabitha and Betty and dropped a coin in the tin marked 'Donations gratefully received'.

On our way we continued, leaving the 'amazing menagerie' as I chose to call it behind. I opened the window of the van and the sun shone through to warm my face and my heart at the same time. We called at Stone Crop Farm – very aptly named, as Mr. Jack Toombs and his brother Jim were acknowledged experts at the art of drystone walling. We passed them on the way up to the farm, two real old troopers sporting straw hats, no shirts (they were brown as berries) and old thick trousers tied up with string round the waist and below the knees. I called to them *"Afternoon Jack, do you want any more Norman Mailer books leaving?"* Jack opened his mouth to reveal his black teeth where he'd sucked his pipes over the years. *"Yes please, and two war books as well please Mrs. Moore. Oh, by the way, if you like whinberries, go up the lane at the right-hand side of the farm, there's some beauties up there."* *"Many thanks,"* I called and we moved up to the farmyard where Mrs. Connie Toombs, in a big flowery apron, brought out a tray full of home-baked shortbread and mugs of coffee. With arms and legs like tree trunks and a back as broad as any man, she was capable of tackling any job on the farm and the Toombs brothers had her well trained. Yet she was a darling, as good hearted as any good countrywoman could be. President of the local WI and a Church Warden as well as Secretary of the PCC, Connie Toombs was loved, hated, feared and respected by all the local community and a friend to all. I asked her if we could collect some whinberries before we left and she readily agreed, even giving me some of the blackcurrants which she'd bottled only that morning. I hurried up the path Jack Toombs had indicated and soon had lots of whinberries as they were large and easy to pick. We thanked Connie and headed for Ramsbottom.

A TASTE OF AUTUMN

September danced in with a twirling of emerald leaves turning first to lime and then to gold. Rural gardens were a riot of crimson and flame as salvias and dahlias competed for the Autumn sunshine. The horse chestnut trees thrilled me, as their leaves changed from green to lemon, then gold, until finally, crimsoned by the late October mists, they reached peak perfection in a glory of vermillion before they cascaded to the floor.

The moors above Darwen and those between Belmont and Abbey Village were a haze of bronzed and caramel coloured bracken blending with the heather. Rosehips and haws ripened and the hedges began to brighten as the sun beat down on them with their bounty of glorious orange and crimson. Roddlesworth Woods below Tockholes became a sheet of flame as the rowan trees produced their annual harvest of bright scarlet berries. The rosebay willow herb lived up to its name of 'fireweed', large patches of it sweeping down the hillsides and wasteland patches around Withnell, Brinscall and Abbey Village. Some people think it's just an ugly, tiresome weed, but I think it's beautiful and adds such a brightness to our towns and villages.

One gorgeous Thursday morning in mid-September, we cruised along the A675 through Belmont village heading for Tockholes. St. Peter's Church at Belmont twinkled in the autumn sunshine and I waved to little Mrs. Ashworth who was cleaning the Post Office window. Some of my Belmont readers were already hurrying about with shopping baskets and string bags, popping into the Co-op shop or standing in the High Street chatting to their neighbours. Mrs. Halliwell from Maria Square was sweeping her flags. Up past the Black Bull we coasted and out towards the turning to Tockholes. The moors were a magnificent ochre colour. The sailing club reservoir on the right was bright with colourful boats waiting for their owners to enjoy them. A kestrel soared high above us, eagerly seeking its prey with a vigilant eye, whilst old Winter Hill, head wreathed with autumnal sunshine, guarded his territory – Rivington, Horwich, Adlington, Blackrod on one side, Bolton and Belmont on the other. We turned right and headed towards Tockholes.

The fir trees on our left stood strong and tall, masters of all they surveyed, whilst further along, the trees of Roddlesworth Woods flaunted their rainbowed glory and harvest of nuts, much to the delight of three grey squirrels who chased each other up and down the trunks and made gigantic leaps from branch to branch. Along the tiny road we trundled until Hollinshead Terrace hove into view and we prepared for our first call of the day. No need to sound the horn for, as Bill reversed round the corner and backed up alongside the houses, doors opened – we had been expected. Across from the terrace were various gardens and allotments and manys the bundle of home-grown rhubarb Bill and I have been given over the years. Grandma Brown was waiting at her door to receive our teapot with the tea already in it. *"Morning love,"* she spoke to me softly, her brown eyes, wizened cheeks and fluffy grey hair giving her the appearance of a little gnome. *"Gladys isn't well today, so would you choose some books for us whilst I brew up, please?"* She took the teapot and disappeared back into No.8.

Meanwhile, Mrs. Garnett and Rose Haworth were perusing the 'New Fiction' section. *"Morning, Mrs. Moore,"* said Rose. *"My George wants something about bee-keeping. Says he's going to start keeping bees in our allotment across the way there. The honey will be nice, but I don't fancy them things buzzing about all over our front room,"* she ventured. I looked for anything we might have on bee-keeping, but could find nothing suitable except a book called *'Me and the Bee'* which was a personal account, so I made a subject request slip for Rose's husband asking for books on bee-keeping.

Mrs. Garnett was deep in conversation with Bill by now. *"Yes, my Jack supports Blackburn Rovers, goes to watch them every week, they've done very well recently, too."* *"Grandma Brown should be ready with the teapot now,"* I told Bill. Taking a pile of books on various subjects and titles, I went into the house. Poor Gladys, her hands and feet were so badly swollen with arthritis that some days she could hardly move, yet she always tried to be cheerful about everything. *"How are you dear? Not too well today? Never mind, I've brought you some nice relaxing books which I hope you'll enjoy."* Gladys smiled at me. *"Thanks love,*

'The Royal' at Tockholes stands four-square to the elements.

once Autumn starts and the damp creeps in, then I start to feel mi joints more." Some 25 years later, living in Rising Bridge, Haslingden, which is beautiful in summer, but very damp and surrounded with chilly mists in autumn and winter, I know exactly what she meant! We chatted amiably until, remembering Bill, I took the teapot into the van and we drank our tea before leaving for the next stop.

No Broomstick or Black Cat.

Down past the 'Royal' pub we chugged, towards 'Pleasant View' cottages, our next stop. Mrs. Emily Fisher was one of our most avid readers who couldn't wait for our arrival. I smiled as I remembered how we'd met her years before when she lived in a little cottage in the woods and had to walk down a steep field to reach the Mobile Library. At that time, Miss Emily Pearson, as she was then, was known to be rather eccentric as she always wore a kind of Scotch Plaid bonnet on her head and a HUGE black cape. When the wind blew under her cape, it billowed out and she had the appearance of a massive bat careering helplessly over the fields and byways. Well, one very windy day in March, we were waiting for Emily on the road at the appointed place, but there was no sign of her at all. I'd just decided she wasn't coming, when I saw her appear at the top of the field complete with black cloak and tartan bonnet. She struggled towards us with obvious difficulty, as the wind was getting quite horrendous! Emily was clasping her cloak round her with one hand and holding her bag of books in the other. The wind roared and Emily was being propelled forward, only just managing to keep upright. Suddenly, a gigantic gust managed to penetrate the back of Emily's cape and she was lifted into the air, bags, books and bonnet flying in all directions and carried for at least twenty yards towards the hedge where we were waiting, like some unidentified flying bomb or missile. We watched open-mouthed and helpless as the poor woman was deposited on top of the hawthorn hedge by the demon wind who seemed to roar with laughter at his misdeed. Both Bill and I burst out laughing. The spectacle of the 'flying bat', as we called her, was like a pantomime to us, with a black witch trying out her flying prowess and the evil wind making a mockery of her. It was too much for us and we both collapsed in a heap behind the van's door. Then we came to our senses and hurried out to help poor Emily.

What a sight she was! Stuck on top of the hedge with her tattered cloak splattered all round her, her face and arms dreadfully scratched. Bill and I extracted her from the hawthorn hedge as carefully as we could. Poor Emily was badly shaken and could hardly stand. *"What are we going to do?"* I asked Bill as I ran up the field to retrieve the bag and library books. In the end, we decided to get Miss Emily into the van and take her down to Tockholes village to find Mrs. Barlow, the local District Nurse. I sat her in my front seat whilst I sat on the floor in the back of the van and we slowly coasted down to West View and Tockholes Post Office. I burst into the homely little shop just as Alice Jones was collecting her pension. *"Have you seen Mrs. Barlow? Is she on her rounds?"* I asked breathlessly. *"What's wrong, Mrs. Moore?"* Little Amy Turner, the postmistress, was full of concern. *"It's Emily Pearson, I'm afraid she's had and accident. Nothing broken, but she's*

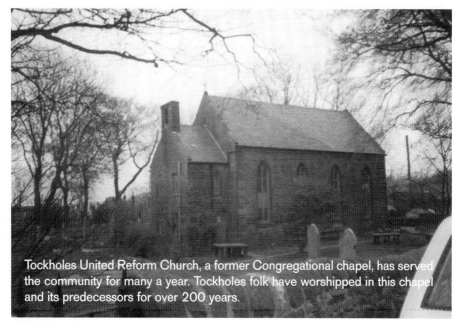

Tockholes United Reform Church, a former Congregational chapel, has served the community for many a year. Tockholes folk have worshipped in this chapel and its predecessors for over 200 years.

been badly shaken," I gasped out. Alice Jones spoke up. *"Mrs. Barlow's at No.9 West View at present. Run up there and you'll catch her,"* she told me. Leaving the two women gasping for more news, I raced up to No.9. Nurse Barlow herself came to the door and I explained what had happened as quickly as I could. *"Keep her in the van and when I've finished this dressing, I'll come and have a look at her,"* she promised.

I went back to the van and Nurse Barlow followed shortly afterwards. Emily was pale and drawn and looked a sorry sight with her face and arms covered with scratches, bruises and blood. Gently, Marion Barlow examined Emily's wounds. What was left of the black cloak was on the library floor. *"Nothing broken,"* said Nurse Barlow, *"but she needs these wounds bathing and treatment for shock. If you can help me get her to my car, Mrs. Moore, I'll take her to my cottage and treat her there. Then I'll go back to her own cottage with her and see she's okay."* Emily Pearson had hardly spoken until now. *"You're so kind, both of you. How can I thank you?"* she uttered. *"Are you sure she'll be alright?"* I asked Nurse Barlow. *"Perfectly, dear. I'll ask Anne Whalley from Pleasant View to call and see her for a few days, I think Emily is friendly with her."* I gave Nurse Barlow Emily's bag and books and she promised she'd let me know next time how Emily was. By this time the van was swarming with curious readers who'd heard that something unusual had happened, so I left Bill to cope for a few minutes whilst we got Emily to Nurse Barlow's car.

As it turned out, Miss Emily herself greeted us two weeks later at the appointed spot and seemed no worse for her ordeal. She thanked us for our help and kind enquiries and said rather sheepishly: *"Everyone said that cloak was a menace and would cause me problems one day, so I've dumped what's left of it and I'll never get another one."* Later, Emily married a widower from Darwen, gave up her cottage and eccentric ways and went to live at Pleasant View cottages as 'Mrs. Walter Fisher' and here she was some years later on this glorious autumnal morning eagerly awaiting our arrival.

"Come here a minute Mrs. Moore, let me show you a lovely sight." I followed Emily round the side of Pleasant View cottages to where there was a patch of moist, beautifully green grass. There, shining brightly in the morning sun, was a sparkling patch of mauve Meadow Saffron or Autumn Crocus, as delicate and perfect as its spring sister. I could hardly speak it was such a wonderful sight to a simple nature lover like me. The mauve flowers were made even more outstanding by their bright orange stamens which contrasted sharply with the lavender petals. I've always loved anything mauve or purple. I think this springs from when I was a child. We had no garden and I was 7 or 8 before I saw my first real crocuses. Their lavender and purple hues were so beautiful and made such an impact on my mind that I've loved these colours ever since. *"I've often seen pictures of them, but I've never actually seen any before,"* I told Emily, who smiled at my delight. In fact, I was so thrilled with the picture of those precious flowers, that I wrote a poem about them when I got home and told my girls of their beauty. Here it is:

Meadow Saffron (Autumn Crocus)

God made the Meadow Saffron
A child of rainbowed hue;
With orange-stamened lavender
And purples streaked with blue.
When crimsoned autumn leaves descend
To mellowed grass, then flow
Look where you put your human tread,
See beauty reached below.
There on the grass in dimpled smile
Wide open to autumnal sun,
A fragile lavendered delight –
Each dew-kissed saffron, every one.
The blackbird sees his chance and steals
A taste of her bright sun warmed flowers,
Only to find they easily break,
Charms vanishing within the hours.
When sunset's blush silences sun
And flurried moonbeams take a peep,
Sweet saffron closes tight her arms
And gently drifts in purpled sleep.

On our way round Tockholes we trundled that sunny morning. Down past West View and the Post Office where our readers cheerfully exchanged news, gossip and views at the same time as changing their books. Then it was down to Ivy Cottages where a bevy of pre-school children swarmed into the van with their mothers to beg for 'Andy Pandy' books and the like. Television programmes for children were only just beginning in the early 1970s, so village children relied on library books a lot more and thoroughly enjoyed them.

Old Misery Guts.

We saw the lovely little church of St. Stephen and went on up the lane past the village school towards that famous pub 'The Rock'. As we waited on the pub car park for customers, I was quietly admiring the view across the moors towards Abbey Village, when there was a great thumping on the van door. I opened it and saw to my dismay the angry face of Israel Miller, the 'misery guts' of Tockholes as he was known behind his back! (Nobody dare call him that to his face) He was a cantankerous old recluse and we'd crossed swords with him before. What was wrong now I wondered. We soon found out! *"Yes, Mr. Miller. Do you want some books?"* I asked carefully. *"Do I hell as like, and what do you mean by knocking down one of my best ewes and not stopping eh?"* Israel thrust his ugly, contorted face close to mine, and I nearly fainted from the smell that eminated from him and his breath which reeked strongly of onions. I was shocked. *"Knocked down one of your sheep. We wouldn't do that Mr. Miller."* *"Yes you did,"* he retorted. *"You were up near the field when it happened – someone saw you, so don't tell lies to me young woman!"* I was flabbergasted and didn't know what to say next, but luckily Bill came to my rescue and leapt to my defence. *"We certainly did not run over your sheep Mr. Miller – we didn't even see one, and if I had knocked one down, I most certainly would have stopped."* *"Well who did then?"* snapped Israel, his face flaring dangerously red. *"I don't know, but it wasn't us,"* replied Bill. Then suddenly, I remembered something. *"Bill, when we were serving Jim Thornton up the road there, didn't a fast car rush past us and we wondered who it was and what it was doing going so fast on a narrow road like this?"* Israel Miller looked slightly less belligerent. *"I suppose it could have been some young loony if it wasn't you,"* he conceded. *"But someone said they saw you,"* he added menacingly. *"Could be they saw us cruising down the lane, but not the fast car zooming past us,"* said Bill. *"Was the sheep killed, by the way?"* *"No – but no thanks to somebody who doesn't give a damn."* Israel seemed to have calmed down a bit and accepted that we weren't the culprits. *"Her legs are broken, but I got her home and the vet is on his way. Anyway, if you see any more fast cars – get their number if you can."* Thus mollified, Israel Miller stomped away back to his sheep.

Time was getting on. We drove towards Pickup Brow where we had two stops, one at the top and one at the bottom for the convenience of our older readers. Our stops completed, we drove along to the crossroads and turned right into what became Bog Height Road. There were two cottages at the top, both with magnificent views over Blackburn and Darwen. We had a customer at 'Moulin Rouge', Mrs.

A recent photograph of Hollinshead Terrace, Tockholes.

Drake, who said that the cottage used to belong to an old lady who'd been a 'Tiller Girl' – hence the name. Mrs. Drake liked whinberries and blackberries as much as I did and told me that if I went down Bog Height Road there were some quite wonderfully huge blackberries there this year. After we'd eaten our sandwiches up on the top road, I walked down to do a bit of blackberry picking whilst Bill had a snooze during our dinner hour.

It was as Mrs. Drake had said, the blackberries were huge, big black beauties glowing in the sun like molten jet. I must have picked about four pounds in no time at all. The family would have blackberry pie and cream this weekend I vowed. Bill yawned and stretched; *"Time we headed for Hoddlesden,"* he told me

Heavenly Hoddlesden.

Hoddlesden had not been one of our villages during my previous years with the Mobile Library, but we had been serving it now for about three years. I was very glad we did too, as the people were so kind and friendly and the scenery was lovely high on the moors up above Darwen. We trundled down Bog Height Road, across the A666 and into Sandy Lane which took us to Lower Darwen. As we chugged up Stopes Brow, I remembered an old lady telling me about sledging down that steep incline on a coal shovel years ago when she was a child. It was quite a struggle for the Mobile Library to reach the crest of the slope near the Royal Ordnance Factory and Bill always sighed with relief when he passed St. James' Church, Blackamoor, on the left. He knew we'd made it! Right at the lights and into Blackamoor Road we turned and headed for Waterside before we stopped at Hoddlesden.

Peter's Paintings.

We had three customers at Waterside, two of them very nice old ladies who seemed to wear wellingtons on their feet all year round. The third was an old man who'd worked at Shaw's Glazed Brickworks for many years. Widowed for some time, he was always trying to entice the two old ladies into his house. I suspected because he was lonely; but they suspected it was because he wanted to tell them all his problems, so they ignored him completely when he came to choose his books. It made things awkward for me when we called with the library, because Ethel Shutt and Mary Porter refused to come into the van whilst Peter Dale was still in it. The conversation went like this: *"Hello Peter." "Hello Mrs. Moore, have you got any new westerns this week?"* I would look on the appropriate shelves for him. Meanwhile, Ethel and Mary would be outside, parading up and down like two peacocks waiting for Peter to leave the van. He spotted them outside the dooor. *"Ethel, Mary, come on in and help me choose something exciting to read, then perhaps you'll come on in and have a cup of tea with me and look at my paintings."* Their faces were stony as they quickly moved away from the open library door. I heard muttered whisperings from outside. *"Silly old faggot, allus trying to get us in that little back room. What would he do if we actually agreed to go?"* Mary said to Ethel. To make a bit of progress, I said to Peter; *"I'll come and see your paintings Peter, if Bill would see to Ethel's and Mary's books."* Bill luckily took the cue and I went outside with Peter, whilst Ethel and Mary mounted the van's steps with some difficulty, glaring at Peter as they went past him. Actually, Peter's paintings were quite good, but the house was permanently cold and dingy and had obviously not seen a woman's touch for years. I felt sorry for him, as he was very lonely and I thought I'd mention him to the vicar of St. Paul's in Hoddlesden, as maybe he could help by getting someone to visit him now and then and give him some company.

Hoddlesden's Heritage.

On we cruised towards Hoddlesden, passing the Vernon-Carus Mill on the left. The firm employed a lot of people from the villages as well as Hoddlesden itself and even workers from Darwen were eager to work there. The usual crowd of readers were waiting for us at the Ranken Arms in the centre of Hoddlesden, head scarves and caps indicating that summer was definitely over.

"Afternoon Mrs. Moore." There was a general chorus of greeting from my readers and a great deal of gossip as well. Hoddlesden has always been a very parochial village, the villagers being proud of their heritage and the fact that they were 'born and bred in Hoddlesden'. A lot of older people were also known by their nicknames, such as 'Tum o' Dick o' Bobs' meaning Tom, son of Dick who was the son of Bob. These names caused Bill and myself great amusement as we were presented with gems like; 'Harry up steps', 'Jessie o' Tripes' or 'Alice up Sough' and were expected to write them on their library tickets.

On this golden afternoon, the readers were full of future village events which all seemed to be connected either with St. Paul's Church or the Congregational

Hoddlesden's Memorial to her dead, an oasis of peace in an already sleepy village.

Chapel. It was the Harvest Festival at St. Paul's that weekend and many of our lady readers were making plans to rob their gardens of colourful flowers to decorate the church. *"I've some lovely dahlias and salvias,"* said Muriel Long. *"My Tom's grown the best chrysanthemums ever – lovely bronze ones too,"* ventured Dot Burns. Mrs. Audrey Woods, President of Hoddlesden WI, took charge as usual: *"We'll all meet at seven on Friday night at the church shall we?"*

I listened with great interest as members of the Chapel offered their flowers and flower-arranging skills to the ladies of St. Paul's. There was a certain amount of rivalry between the two denominations, yet they came together to help celebrate special occasions and anniversaries.

One in the Oven.

Mr. Bunn, the local baker (a very appropriate name you'll agree), was making the big 'sheaf of corn' loaf as he did every year and the good ladies of Hoddlesden would provide parkin, currant cake, fruit loaves, fruit pies, and many other goodies for the Harvest Supper, I was assured. How I loved hearing about all these church socials: Harvest Suppers, 'Rose Queen at Homes', Afternoon Teas, Beetle and Whist Drives, Sunday School Concerts and the other social events which contributed so much to village life. I was pleased to note that the 'Ladies Aid' group and Mother's Union members had strong followings as well.

There was also much talk in many of the villages we visited about Processions of Witness, commonly known as 'Walking Days', and I listened enthralled as the mothers of the 'Rose Queens' and 'Sunday School Queens' who were to lead the processions made plans for their offspring – often making the dresses and robes themselves. People were far more self-reliant then and not as dependent on commercialism! My own two daughters were both Rose Queens at St. John's, Stonefold, and we had a 'Walking Day' there up until the 1990s which everybody enjoyed at that time. Today, however, the talk at Hoddlesden centred on the Harvest Supper at St. Paul's and the Misses Hindle were debating whether to wear their blue or brown dresses. Felt hats and gloves were a must for any social occasion in those days.

The village of Hoddlesden was lovely, with many tiny houses and cottages which the villagers took great pride in keeping clean and spotless, inside and out. Alice Walsh, a retired school teacher, enjoyed reading and never failed to visit us every fortnight. *"I like the country tales best,"* she informed me, *"but I feel I could write a book on my own experiences,"* she volunteered. *"Why don't you then? I'm sure you've many humorous experiences to relate,"* I urged her. A couple from Browning Street whom I'd never seen before entered the van. *"What's this then?"* asked the man. *"Have the Co-op started a book service?"* *"Sorry, it's not the Co-op, it's a service provided for you by the County Council,"* I explained. *"Oh! I thought it was only t' Co-op as come round wi vans,"* he exclaimed. *"No, we're here to serve you as best we can and if there's any particular book you want, just ask me,"* I encouraged him. His wife was perusing the shelves carefully. *"I like Jean Plaidy, have you her latest?"* she asked. I looked and found what was the latest on the shelves. *"Thanks very much,"* said Mrs. Tickle, for that was her name, and so the ice was broken and a firm friendship begun. On subsequent visits I was treated to tales of Harold Moore, Mrs. Tickle's grandad, who'd been champion clog fighter of Hoddlesden for many years. If anyone doubts that the vicious sports of clog and cock fighting did take place, then they should contact some of the older residents of Hoddlesden and Darwen whose ancestors enjoyed taking part in this kind of local entertainment and passed down the gory details to astonished members of their families. Mrs. Tickle was a darling, just like her namesake; full of fun with twinkling eyes that missed nothing; her descriptions of her grandfather's legs after he'd been in a clog fight had me in tucks!

Up the road we went, passing what were then open fields, but are now estates of pleasant modern houses whose occupants still frequent the Mobile Library. It was getting a little cooler but the autumn sun was gilding the top of Darwen Moor and spreading a glow across the little town in the valley.

We are a Community Service.

We turned left at the crossroads into Blacksnape Road and headed for Ramsbottom, passing the tiny chapel of St. Mary's, Grimehills, just before the 'Crown and Thistle' on that nasty little bend, so difficult to negotiate. We were just cruising along nicely, enjoying the pleasant autumn sunshine and dropping down past Widdup's Farm, carefully monitoring the steep dip, when suddenly, quite out of the blue, something black hurled itself in front of us. Bill slammed on the brakes and I jolted forward as the thunder of two-thousand books cascading onto the floor hit my ears. *"What on earth?"* I began, rubbing my head which hurt from the bump it had received! Bill jumped out of the van and went round the front to see what had happened. In front of the wheel on the driver's side lay the body of what used to be a beautiful farm dog. As I joined Bill, I could see blood oozing from a gash on the dog's head. *"There's nothing we can do for him – he's dead,"* said Bill. *"We must find the owner,"* I stressed, *"I'll go back up the hill to the cottages and ask there."* I'd no need to move, because at that moment we heard the sound of running feet and a voice shouting, *"Ben, where are you?"* A lady I didn't recognise came into view round the side of the van, and when she saw the lifeless body in front of the wheel she fell down on her knees and began to sob. *"Ben, oh my poor Ben..."* She looked up at us, her face awash with tears and said in a broken voice *"It's my fault, I left the door open by mistake and when he gets a chance, he runs out looking for my husband who died recently. You see, he was Jack's dog, and he still can't understand why he doesn't come home any more, so at every opportunity he goes looking for him. Oh, why did I forget to close the door?"* Tears poured down her face as she stroked the rough hair and bleeding head, but there was no response from the prostrate body. I forgot about the books lying on the library floor as I looked at the distraught woman who knelt by Ben's body. Bill's voice was gentle as he got out our old blanket and threw it over Ben. *"Let me carry him home for you, then maybe someone will bury him for you. Do you live far from here?"* *"What? Oh, sorry, no. I'm Mrs. Haworth and I live in one of those cottages behind the farm back there."* She indicated some buildings behind us on the left. An angry toot behind us indicated that we'd left the van still obstructing the road. I went to explain what had happened to the frustrated motorist, whilst Bill first moved Ben to the side of the road, then pulled the van over to allow traffic to pass. The red car started up and moved forward, the driver somewhat mollified by my account of the tragedy. Bill came back to Mrs. Haworth, scooped Ben, now wrapped in our old blanket, into his arms and resolutely marched up the hill with Mrs. Haworth leading the way. I decided I'd better start to put the books back on the shelves!

All this had taken some time, of course, and when I looked at my watch, I was surprised to see that it was almost 4-45pm and we were due in Ramsbottom at 5-00pm. No chance of getting all the books back on the shelves and in the right order, I reflected! A few minutes later, Bill joined me in the van. *"She's terribly upset – I didn't like to leave her, but her neighbour came in and promised to stay with her".* *"She asked if we'd any damage to the van, which we haven't outside, but I didn't tell her about all this in here,"* he said, ruefully glancing at the books on the floor. *"Well,"* I began, *"I don't think there's any point in us trying to get all these in order tonight – for one thing, we're in a bad place on the road and for another, Ramsbottom Library will be closed by the time we get there."*

I suggested we drive back with the books as they were and put them back on the shelves before we started for Belmont Village tomorrow. Clambering into our front seats we drove back to base. Anna Jackson was suitably sympathetic when I told her why we were so late and said we were right to act as a 'community – not just a library' service.

About a week later, Miss Jackson received a phone call from Mrs. Haworth asking her to thank us for our help, and could she become a member of the Mobile Library and borrow some books? We duly found room for her on the appropriate route, and she became one of our readers, acquiring for herself another 'Ben' a few weeks later. *"We do have some strange ways of finding new readers, don't we?"* I said to Bill as we spent the rest of the autumn days coasting happily round the country lanes and byways.

IN THE BLEAK MID WINTER

We certainly had some mixed winters in the early 1970s. No two winters were alike – and they definitely weren't as bad as the ones in the 1940s when I was a child. I can clearly remember 1947 when the snow at our house in Oswaldtwistle was half-way up the downstairs window; Green Haworth and Gaulkthorn were cut-off from everything for three weeks.

No, the winters Bill and I experienced ranged from the relatively mild falls of snow which soon disappeared, to the biting east winds when the snow froze on the windscreen of the van and we skidded and slewed on the farm tracks. My readers, bless their hearts, always greeted winter in the same way. They never changed their philosophies and attitudes. These, my 'Lancashire Natives', had survived hardship and poverty which stood them in good stead for later life, and most of them lived to a ripe old age in spite of lack of money and material possesions.

"Lap up well"

It was always the same. As soon as the weather 'turned', as Mrs. Gabbott of Belthorn put it, I noticed that all my readers became much fatter. This was due to the fact that they entrenched themselves in at least three pullovers or sweaters. Woollen hats pulled well down over the ears became the order of the day and up in Belthorn village, new balaclavas were hastily knitted. There was also much talk about *"This new thermal underwear stuff as is cum about,"* Mrs. Brindle told me. *"I've had a terrible back,"* she reiterated, *"so I'm thinkin' o' geddin' one o' them theer 'mummy' things as keeps yer back warm. I've sin it in one o' yon catalogues fra' Yorkshire."* I puzzled for a long time about the 'mummy'. *"Whatever's one of those?"* I asked several Belthorn veterans as they paraded round the van in thick overcoats and long skirts. Nobody in Belthorn seemed to know, but the answer came surprisingly from a pensioner at Edgworth who told me she'd got a 'body warmer' for the same purpose of keeping her back and 'middle parts' warm. Round the villages we slipped and slithered, braving the ice and snow to serve our readers from an area which stretched from Brinscall and Withnell Fold at one end, to the bleak moors of Blackstone Edge and Littleborough at the other. Sometimes we had to miss farms because the roads were too slippery or dangerous, but this wasn't often. I was amused to see the washing lines full of frozen bloomers, vests and combinations – some of them enormous in size, blowing in the cruel winter winds. *"The misses Scarlett and Opal Sandys are back to their flannelette nighties and wincyette bloomers,"* I observed as we slithered past their cottage. There was very little central heating in the village homes in those days, so it was still mostly coal fires in our readers' domains. Many's the bitterly cold winter's day when I was invited into someone's cottage for *"A warm-up and a cup of Oxo love."*

Peeks at Our Peaks.

As always, the hills and moors looked beautiful when they were covered with a sprinkling of snow and so I forgave the evil weather and the disasters it could cause as we drove through Edgworth up to Entwistle and I saw the wild white beauty surrounding me. Winter Hill, majestic as ever and exceptionally magnificent with a crown of snow, was a landmark not to be missed in his winter splendour. When we visited our readers above Oswaldtwistle, well then it was 'Old Pendle' who had the crown of snow then.

An Overnight Stay.

We managed to survive the winters very well, except for one year, when in January at about four in the afternoon as we were returning from Brinscall, freezing fog caused us to abandon the Mobile Library in a lay-by and seek shelter at a nearby farm. Fortunately, Mrs. Astley was one of our readers and she readily gave us shelter for the night, but we had to use the Police phone at Belmont to contact Ramsbottom Library and our own homes.

The Good Samaritans.

This particular January seemed to have been exceptionally cold, with a lot of snow and ice, the vicious wind icing the windscreen of the Mobile Library so much that some days we could hardly manage to drive a short distance before we couldn't see at all for the frozen snow and ice on the windscreen. On one such day, we'd been up to Archer's Farm and were on our way across the moorland roads, when the windscreen became so frozen that we had to stop and clean it. Bill was engaged in his task and I was busy trying to keep warm outside the van door, when I heard a faint cry. The wind was absolutely 'fleeing' and I pulled my hood closer round my ears. Then – there it was again, a faint cry from behind the wall where we were stopped. I looked over the wall and gasped, for there was a sheep on its side and it was just giving birth to a tiny lamb. The cruel wind was so cold that the blood and afterbirth matter on the unfortunate infant was freezing on its body before the mother could lick it clean. I called *"Bill, come here quickly and look at what I've found."* Bill came and looked over the wall and took in the situation at a glance. *"What are we to do?"* I asked. *"The lamb will die in this wind."* We couldn't see a farm anywhere around, but I knew we needed to act quickly. I went in the van and found the old blanket we kept for all kinds of emergencies, then I climbed over the wall and gathered the lamb into its folds and carried it into the van. Bill helped the mother ewe to scramble to her feet and she seemed none the worse for her ordeal, but he dusted the snow off her coat and gave her some bread to eat anyway.

Inside the van, the tiny lamb stirred in my arms and snuggled into the blanket, but I knew she'd need food and treatment as soon as possible. Bill got back into the van and looked around the bleak landscape. *"There must be a farm somewhere.*

Let's go on for a bit along this road and see if we can find one," I said to him. The windscreen had been cleared, so we trundled along the road looking for a farm which could help the newly born lamb. Eventually a plume of smoke on the left indicated a farm was near. We found the track and hurried up towards the farm as fast as we dared. The farmer's wife came to the door, astonished at our arrival, as it turned out she new nothing about our library service! I jumped out of the door, the lamb wrapped in the blanket in my arms. Mrs. Betty Plant listened to my tale and ushered us into the kitchen where she carefully examined the animal. *"She's not one of ours, I don't think,"* she said, *"as we've no ewes so far advanced in lambing. But you did right to bring her here, with this icy wind, she'd surely have died otherwise. Where exactly was the sheep?"* she asked Bill, as she placed the lamb in front of her glowing, cheerful fire. Bill told her as best he could, whilst we, glad of the warmth, monopolised the radiant heat. *"Hmmn, could be one of Cyril Walsh's,"* mused Betty. *"He's just along the road at Three Brooks Farm. I'll give him a ring. Would you like a cup of Oxo?"* - Would we not!

Bill and I stood in front of the fire drinking our Oxos, the infant lamb revelling in the unaccustomed heat. Betty Plant went to phone her neighbour and came back smiling. *"Yes, Cyril thinks one of his ewes could have given birth and from the directions you've given of where you've found her, its nearly sure to be his lamb. He's coming over right now, can you wait to see him, he wants to thank you personally?"* I glanced at Bill. We only had three more farms to visit before heading back to Ramsbottom and the farmers weren't going to be outside in the cold waiting for us, so I nodded in the affirmative. Betty Plant took a soft cloth dipped in warm water and began to clean the lamb's face and body. Yet, funnily enough, as soon as she'd started, her old sheepdog, Bonnie, ambled over, settled down next to the lamb and began to lick it clean all over. *"Well!"* exclaimed Betty, *"I never expected that to happen. Bonnie's been a good mother in the past, but she's too old for pups now. Maybe she misses having them and she seems to be enjoying playing mother to the little lamb, doesn't she?"* Bill and I smiled at the old dog and Betty took away her cloth and water and left Bonnie to it!

Minutes later, there was a knock at the door and Farmer Walsh strode in. A huge man, with a weatherbeaten face and crinkly blue eyes which smiled gratefully at us, he swooped down on the precious lamb and held it close. *"Yes, I think it's one of mine. I've just seen one of my ewes full of blood which looks like she's given birth, as she was pregnant,"* he explained. *"I'm very grateful to you for your quick thinking. This wind is so cold the lamb wouldn't have lasted ten minutes if you hadn't saved her!"* *"I'm just glad we did the right thing,"* I said. Cyril Walsh gave us a clean old blanket as he said ours was ruined, and he watched Bonnie mothering the lamb when he put her back on the rug for a few minutes. *"Cleaned her up nicely, she has,"* he told us, *"sheep dogs are very good mothers and I've seen quite a few mother new-born lambs as well."* Cyril then picked up the lamb for the last time, wrapped safely in our old blanket ready to take back to Three Brooks Farm, but not before he'd given Bill and myself a dozen fresh brown eggs *"Newly laid this morning, and many thanks once again."*

72

A New Recruit.

Mrs. Plant questioned us about our library service: *"I'd like to join if that's possible. Can you fit me into your schedule?"* she asked. I assured her that we could, by rearranging the times of visits to the other farms, so she chose some books for all her family and we drove to the next farm. We were, of course, later than usual, but I explained why to our readers and they were all very interested in the tale of the neighbour's lamb. *"Never known one as early afore,"* said old George Hudson. Incidentally, after joining the library, every time we visited Mrs. Plant, she relayed details of 'Tilly', the lamb we'd rescued. Tilly grew up to be well and healthy after being fed and housed in Cyril Walsh's kitchen until the weather improved. She was reunited with her real mother sometime later.

The intense cold continued. Ponds and lakes froze, even some of the tiny moorland streams froze round the edges as well which was unusual. Wayoh and Entwistle Reservoirs became shimmering pools of ice and it was fun to see Canada Geese and Eider Ducks slipping and sliding across their surfaces. The poor birds were frantic with hunger and I purposely took bags of bread, buns and wild bird seed out with me. These were shared between the moorhens, the birds on the reservoirs and the tiny hopefuls who flocked round our van every time we stopped. What a variety of birds we had; robins, thrushes, blackbirds, starlings, jays, blue, great, coal and long tailed tits, greenfinches, chaffinches – all so desperate for food that they came right up to the door of the van whistling and bobbing, begging for even a crumb or two. I was thrilled to see them so close and was delighted to be able to help them.

A Pheasant Surprise.

One bitter day up in Belmont village, I had to call at a house in Waterfall Terrace to collect some books from an elderly reader who couldn't come to the van. Leaving Bill to attend to the other readers, I walked carefully down the slippery street and rounded the corner of Waterfall Terrace. As I did so, I got a shock for there on the wall which runs at the front of the cottages and separates them from the trees and water below was an enormous cock pheasant – beautifully coloured and displaying himself in the mild sunshine! I don't know who got the biggest surprise, me or the poor bird, as in my black balaclava hat, huge sheepskin coat and tartan pants, the bird probably wondered what freak of nature or kind of creature stood before him, as he'd probably never seen anything quite like me dressed in my cold weather gear before! For a moment we eyed each other carefully in breathless silence, me admiring the beauty of this magnificent bird and he probably wondering what I was and if I was going to do him any harm. I stood stock still and wished I'd had my camera with me. He took one last look at my strange apparrel and, with a flick of his magnificent tail, flopped over the wall to the safety of the grass and trees below. Much cheered by this unique meeting, I collected the books and returned to the van to help Bill with the rest of the work.

Belthorn Post Office, in Holden Street, a delightful row of cottages just off the village's main street.

Dressed for the Weather.

Day after day the frost continued; it was certainly weather for thick sweaters, thermal underwear, combinations, fur hats, coats and gloves. I was inundated with offers and gifts of scarves, thick woollen hats, balaclavas, mittens, gloves, socks, waiscoats, a myriad of hand knitted garments, all meant to help me keep warm. My readers, bless their warm Lancashire hearts, were experts at knitting all kinds of body-warming apparel and they wanted to make sure that I was warm enough on my journeys in the Mobile Library. Mrs. O'Shea, one of my readers from Turton who kept a lot of livestock as well as geese, swans, ducks and hens etc. had decided that her hens weren't laying properly *"...because their heads are too cold, the poor things,"* she told me. So she'd knitted each hen a little yellow bonnet which tied around their necks with tape. The first time I saw them, I opened the van door and nearly fell out I laughed so much. There must have been about 20 white leghorns running about and scratching at the frozen grass, their heads bobbing up and down clad in these yellow bonnets. Yet, they didn't seem to mind them at all and strutted round, yellow heads held high and eyes alert piercing through the gloom of the wool. Mrs. O'Shea noticed my mirth: *"Oh yes, they do look funny, but they've laid more eggs since their heads have been warm,"* she told me. As she also regarded these hens as pets, having an individual name for each one of them, she was more sensitive to their needs than most people would have been.

In Sheep's Clothing.

One very cold morning in one of the villages, I had my red balaclava on, knitted for me by Maggie Brunshaw, one of our most avid readers. I'd been a little startled by its thickness and bright colour when she'd presented it to me. *"Ter keep yer head warm love,"* she bellowed, as she was rather deaf. However, it was lovely and warm and did a good job of protecting my head and ears from the intense cold. But, this particular morning, an elderly reader by the name of Walter Woolf came into the van and, seeing my red head remarked; *"Well, if it isn't 'Little Red Riding Hood' we've got this morning eh?"* All my readers were agog to hear what I'd say. So, thinking quickly, I replied; *"Yes, and here comes the 'Big Bad Woolf' to molest me."* A shout of laughter greeted my reply, as I don't suppose Walter Woolf had ever thought about his name, but it made me think twice about putting on that red balaclava again!

My readers didn't confine themselves to knitting outer garments either. They also knitted thick vests, knickers, men's underpants and long johns, body warmers and what they called 'back belts'; *"To keep t'bottom of yer back warm, dear,"* Mrs. Jackson informed me.

Was Joseph's Coat Made in Lancashire?

As there was no bar on colours, there were some horrendous combinations of wools of different hues. *"To use up our odds n' ends, dear,"* Mrs. Fairburn of Oakwood cottages told me. She was one of my favourite readers, and had trouble with her white wispy hair which she tried vainly to pile up into a bun on top of her head. As she also sported a purple bonnet decorated with pink stripes on top of her hair concoction, the effect was ludicrous, to say the least. Mrs. Fairburn was so sweet natured that she was oblivious to the amusement that her appearance caused. Similarly, there were combinations of scarlet and purple, orange and pink, green and vivid yellow, all knitted in a profusion of hats, gloves, scarves and the like. One exceptionally cold day, little Mrs. Miller took me aside and whispered; *"Could you do with this dear?"* A brown paper bag was pressed into my hand and on opening it, out fell the most prodigious pair of purple and yellow knickers I'd ever seen! I held them aloft for all the readers to see and they, like me, burst out laughing. Cold I might be, but there was no way I was going to wear those horrors. However, I didn't want to offend kind Mrs. Miller, so I thanked her for them and put them back in the bag, telling her I'd wear them next week. I was also given an orange body warmer, some vivid green socks and a yellow vest. I accepted them gratefully, but on showing them to my husband and daughters at home, they caused great amusement.

Towards the end of the month, however, it did become a little warmer and thankfully, we stopped slipping and sliding on icy patches and could travel more easily. One lovely, bright sunny day, we were travelling along the A675 between Belmont and Abbey Village. It was exciting to see just a sprinkling of snow on Winter Hill and the moors; what a pretty sight! Just off the A674 Blackburn to Chorley road was the tiny hamlet of Withnell Fold, it was so picturesque, I couldn't believe how lovely it was. It has since been made into a Conservation Area with new houses. There was a bitter wind which managed to find its wicked way into our ears and necks, in spite of extra warm clothing, but the sun was shining brightly and slivers of ice twinkled at us from the holly bushes as we trundled down to the little Methodist Church which was our first stop. Little Miss Fearn came in and asked; *"Have you any new Georgette Heyer's dear, as I've read all the one's in the the van?"* *"Not at present, but I'll get you some for next time,"* I promised.

Cheered by the prospect of a warm drink ahead, we arrived at the little square of cottages known simply as 'Withnell Fold'. How charming they were, all beautifully maintained with picturesque gardens full of snowdrops and tiny yellow aconites, with one or two early crocuses beginning to bud. The old paper mill was still there, although I was told it had ceased production about 1968. The mill had been famous for good quality paper and the mill manager's house was also still there, next to a farm where swallows flooded back in the spring. Our readers were waiting for us and were eager to choose their books, no doubt glad to get back to the warmth of their cosy cottages. There was much grumbling about backache, cold winds and pains in the neck and joints, but as they were normally such warm-hearted and generous people, I smiled at them indulgently and ignored their grumbles. *"I can afford to allow them a bit of acrimony now and then,"* I thought as I watched them examining the latest additions to our stock.

Mrs. Best entered the van with a tray full of beakers of coffee and home-baked biscuits; as she had her young grand-daughter in tow, I said I would return the tray later. How we enjoyed that hot sweet liquid as old Mrs. Johnson decided between a Catherine Cookson or a Susan King. I jumped out of the van to return the cups to Mrs. Best. As I came round the corner, the sight which met my eyes quite took my breath away, for there, round four or five of the tiny porches and doors, the pale lemon flowers of the Winter Jasmine were glinting in the January sunshine. Their frail flowers and stems twined slender arms around the porches and doors, the delicate blossoms bravely defying the icy winds and I marvelled at

Marie behind the counter of her shop in Bury Lane, Withnell, serving Alice Martin in March 1995.

the strength of such fragile beauty! I tried to describe the scene to my daughters when I got home, but it was impossible to convey to them the wonder of something so delightful, so I wrote a poem about it instead. Here it is.

Winter Jasmine

Flower of December – heaven sent
To brighten winter's cold lament.
Your pulsing buds burst forth and glow –
Then your secret gold you will show.
Sweeping upwards from cold earth
Bright golden blossoms then give birth.
Reaching out towards the sky
Our cottage doors you beautify.
Winter Jasmine, yellow flowers unwrapping,
On the cottage window tapping,
Starring the walls with your golden charms,
Whispering softly in nature's arms.
Earliest flower of the year
You bring us joy in winter's drear.

She Breast-fed the British Army.

After we'd served all the readers at Withnell Fold, we continued towards Higher Wheelton. We'd had a request from a Mrs. Nodding who lived near Jenny Lane if we could fit her into the schedule. Always happy to oblige, we stopped at a convenient point near to her house. Mrs. Nodding! With a name like that I imagined a dear, sweet, grey-haired lady complete with steel curlers, hairnet and shawl. What a shock I got when she stormed into the van – she should have been called 'Mrs. Booming' instead! An enormous lady – all of 17 stone with breasts like cow's udders flapping above her ample stomach. (*"Had she never heard of foundation garments?"* I wondered) *"NOW"* she boomed as her feet thundered down on an innocent and unfortunate beetle exploring the library's floor. *"NOW! Let me tell you what I want to read."* I stood listening, open-mouthed as an endless list of authors and titles flowed from her lips. We didn't have half of what she wanted, but I did my best to oblige from the stock I had. The pile of books on the desk grew higher and higher. I protested faintly, *"Haven't you got enough books yet? We'll be here again in two weeks."* *"Is this going to be your usual time?"* Mrs. Nodding demanded, *"I would prefer half an hour later."* *"Well,"* I ventured, *"we've tried hard to fit you into the schedule and it's the best we can do at present."* *"I will try to get here every fortnight, but I can't promise to be on time every visit."* In her purple pants and tangerine jumper she looked a formidable opponent.

She rapped imperiously on the counter. *"One more thing, I'm a GREEN enthusiast, and I would like some books on GREEN issues."* She said the word

GREEN with a loud hiss so that she made sure we heard her and knew exactly what she meant! I promised to do my best. Mrs. Nodding had turned her attention back to the bookshelves. She was not put off by my protests at the number of books she'd amassed and continued to haul novels and non-fiction alike off the shelves like a recluse let loose in a supermarket! I don't know how long she'd have stayed if Bill hadn't taken the initiative and started the engine shouting; *"Sorry madam, but we do have to get to the next stop now as people will be waiting."* Whereupon Mrs. Nodding banged down the books she'd got in her arms and I took out the tickets as quickly as possible before she took any more. *"We'll have trouble with her if we're not careful,"* said Bill as we raced towards Higher Wheelton school.

"MERRY CHRISTMAS, MRS. MOORE, MERRY CHRISTMAS, BILL."

After the dull mists and incessant rains of a cold November, December sparkled in, a flurry of snow flakes and a twinkling of frost on country lane verges and meadows. Puddles and shallow ponds were soon frozen over and I enjoyed watching the wild ducks and starlings slipping, sliding and scrambling on the ice as we ate our lunch in the Mobile Library with the heater on. The poor little moorhens were devastated by this unaccustomed unavailability of food and water. I'd been especially vigilant of a pair on a small pond near Greens Arms Road and had observed their progress over the past months. Five chicks had fledged in June, but only two had survived as far as I could see. I wondered what had become of them, as now only the parents remained and I know that there is only so much food for these shy birds in one area. On this Monday morning in early December, we were glad to accept the proferred cups of coffee, Oxo or Bovril which our friends were always ready to make for us. We'd visited Round Barn at 10am and had worked our way down towards Edgworth calling at various farms and cottages on the way. As we later approached the frozen pond near Greens Arms Road, I saw the little moorhens vainly scrabbling for food in the frozen rushes. I had just the thing for them and hurried out with a bag of wild bird food and some buns which I'd saved from last week's baking. I threw down the food, then watched from the van window as the timid birds cautiously approached it. They ate eagerly and I was sure this was the first food they'd tasted for some days, so ever after that, each time we passed the pond I made sure I'd some food with me for the moorhens. Home made buns and cakes may not be ideal food for wild birds, but if it helps them in the struggle through the winter – does it really matter?

December days were cold but beautiful – bright, sunny, golden mornings, trees glinting with tiny crystals of frost and snow and the fiery red sunsets brightening the Lancashire hills with a crimson glory. As we forged our way along country lanes and through parochial villages, the holly trees gleamed with a newly polished look on every leaf, the crimson berries complementing the dark green. Thrushes, blackbirds and chaffinches carolled loudly and I rewarded them with my home-made fayre.

Of course, my readers were full of talk about preparations for Christmas. There was much whispering about whether or not 'Fred' needed black or navy socks; did 'John' want a pullover or did 'Elsie' really need any more hand-knitted bed-socks? Balls of wool were surreptitiously exchanged from wicker basket to wicker basket amidst furtive nods and glances. I watched all this with tolerant amusement, especially as I knew from past experience that I'd be the recipient of at least some of these hand-knitted home-produced gifts. The butcher's in Brinscall had a big notice in the window: "Order your fresh turkey now. Free chestnut stuffing with all orders placed before December 17th". Mrs. George, who lived in Bury Lane, Withnell, told me of how when she was young her father had won a huge goose from his works' Christmas Draw. *"Trouble was,"* she said, *"it was still alive and poor soft-hearted father couldn't bear to kill it. In the end, a neighbour put its neck in his front door and banged it shut. That did the trick, but we children cried, because we were up all night helping mother pluck the thing to use the feathers for an eiderdown and pillows, and they were all over the house. Then, when she did get the bird trussed-up and prepared, it was too big to fit into our old oven and boiler, so it had to be cooked in the big oven at the mill. I couldn't eat any of it at all though, it was such a beautiful bird, I thought it was a shame to kill it. I think that goose lasted us for weeks!"*

Domestic Bliss.

Other readers were less enthralled by the 'Magic of Christmas' and grumbled constantly about the work it made. *"Med mi write over 50 cards mi wife did,"* said Bob Place of Tockholes. *"Then, as if that weren't enough, she med mi walk round and deliver 'em as well. Then, I'd to spend two nights helpin' her mek trimmings an' paper chains. Then, I'd to put 'em all up for her! Missed nearly four nights at the Royal,"* he grumbled. Just then, Jenny, Bob's wife, appeared; he quickly shut up and searched the library shelves very diligently. Personally I have always enjoyed making trimmings, especially 'Cat-Steps' where you have two or three different kinds of coloured crepe paper cut into strips and then keep folding and turning them to make a very pretty Christmas decoration to hang from ceiling and walls. My two young daughters would spend hours trimming not only the Christmas tree, but every single room of the house, especially their bedrooms, with cotton wool snow, holly, ivy, evergreens, mistletoe and of course 'Cat-Steps'.

Recipes Reciprocated.

Many well tried and tested recipes were exchanged between old friends in the comfort of the library van as well as at their own firesides. The vicar's wife at Belmont asked if I'd like her to make me one of her special Christmas puddings, which were the talk of Belmont WI. As my Christmas puddings were as heavy as lead, I thought it a good idea. I may be able to make buns for the birds, but I am told my culinary efforts are not as good as my writings! One of my favourite readers, Mrs. Dooley, gave me a delicious recipe for a lemon crumble which I tried to make, but didn't succeed very well as it was hard and lumpy – not a bit like the mouth-watering piece I'd been given by her. Miss Marigold Masham, that bastion of goodwill, knowing my love of mauve and purple, gave me a striped purple scarf she'd knitted herself.

The crossroads at Edgworth, Whiteheads butcher's shop has its front door on the corner of the sturdy building of locally-quarried stone. The cast-iron fingerpost was erected by Turton Urban District Council, which had the largest acreage in the county - second largest in the country.

Support Home Industries.

As Christmas Day drew near, so the village shops and Post Offices twinkled with fairy lights, snow scenes and other displays to tempt would-be customers to shop locally. In the early 1970s, the supermarket had not yet managed to gain a hold in these rural communities, and a lot of shopping was still 'local'. The Post Office at Hawkshaw had a very realistic Nativity scene, whilst the grocers concentrated on large displays of chocolates and biscuits. At Edgworth Post Office, the music of 'Jingle Bells' rang forth each time the door was opened and the bells were set jingling by the draught. Across the road, the butcher and grocer had 'Special Xmas Offers', including the butcher's home-made, special, secret recipe pork and beef sausages. The Co-op (they had a shop at Belmont village for example) competed valiantly for extra Christmas trade and I was told by Marigold Masham that their own jellies and jams were far superior to any other she'd ever tasted. Tiny Christmas trees, bedecked with miniature robins and fairy lights appeared in the rural cottage windows and also in the rows of houses along the road through Abbey Village. Lily Marsden's shop did a roaring trade and in nearby Brinscall, Hull's grocers were offering their own make of special Christmas mincemeats. Those twin terrors, the Misses Scarlett and Opal Sandys were scathing of such shop-bought rubbish. *Always made our own pies, custards, Christmas puddings,*

Christmas cakes, jams, marmalades, cakes and bread," Miss Scarlett told me in no uncertain terms. *"Too lazy to bake, some of them these days,"* her sister pronounced as she sniffed loudly and stomped round the van sending pads of snow off her boots onto the floor! As she'd just given me a jar of her home-made marmalade *"...for your good service and kind help, dear,"* I said nothing. Later, when my family has actually eaten the marmalade and declared it delicious, I complimented her on her preserving skills and agreed with her about home-made food tasting better.

Time was closing in on both my readers and myself. We were all very, very busy. Not many people had freezers in the early 1970s, so shopping had to be done only a few days before the great day. We were now starting on the last fortnightly rota on the run up to the Christmas break; the van would be off the road for seven days over the Christmas period. My warm-hearted, generous readers did not forget our small service and we were inundated with gifts of puddings, Christmas cakes, bottles of home-made wine and a myriad of carefully wrapped parcels which were slipped into my hand or placed modestly on the table where I discharged the books. I retained some of the wrapped parcels to open on Christmas Day with my family, but some I opened at once, as I was urged to do so by their beaming owners. *"I do hope you like these,"* said little Mrs. Baron, as yet another pair of mittens was added to the pile I had back at Rising Bridge. *"I knitted them in purple especially for you,"* said Emma Crow as a pair of purple monsters was divulged. Felt and cloth pin cushions, sewing books, lace mats beautifully executed, book marks made of pressed flowers, various pieces of tatting and embroidery, manufactured sewing kits and many, many more useful items which my unselfish, caring readers gave as a token of their appreciation. Of course, some of them weren't really much use, but I accepted them all gratefully and indeed, to this day, I still have some of these gifts here in my home to remind me of my very happy days spent serving the 'Rural Readers of Lancashire'.

Bill and I reciprocated and gave boxes of chocolates or other gifts to those of our readers who so thoughtfully gave us hot drinks and ginger biscuits in winter and iced lemonade in summer. The Misses Alice and Martha Berry of Ryefield Avenue, Belmont, were two such people who never failed to assuage our thirst at any time of the year and I never visited Belmont village without calling on them long after I'd finished work on the Mobile Library. (Mrs. Molly Woods of Chapeltown Road, Turton, a very sprightly 80-plus, still makes a brew for the current library driver in 1996.)

On December 15th, we had visited a lot of farms in the morning, followed by visits to Garsden Avenue, Knuzden, and then back to Duckworth Hall and the Britannia Inn. There was ice on the roads making them dangerously slippery and Bill took extra care as we drove along past Ye Olde Brown Cow and on to Ramsclough Farm. Kind Mrs. Whitworth gave us each a cup of coffee as the skies darkened and freezing rain splattered on the windscreen. *"Better hurry home as soon as you've been to Cross Edge and Green Haworth,"* Mrs. Whitworth commented. Bill wasted no time in scooting along to the 'Shoulder of Mutton' and the cluster of houses around it where a few faces appeared at windows and doors as Bill blew the horn to announce our arrival. Green Haworth Chapel stood in all its glory, stoically defying the wind and rain to defend its heritage. Years ago, that famous local lad, the Rev. Jimmy Butterworth, who founded Boys' Clubs, used to preach there and people came from miles around to hear him. On this dark and dull December day, the chapel brooded silently in the gathering dusk and I remembered the many Anniversary Services and Afternoon Tea Socials which had been held there years ago. We left Cross Edge and trundled back towards the A677 which runs between Haslingden and Blackburn, calling at one or two farms and houses along the way. Mrs. Hindle, from 'Red Walls', wished us a *"Merry Christmas,"* and deposited a small parcel on the table. *"For you to enjoy with your coffee."* She nodded at Bill and departed towards her front door. I opened the parcel – it was some home-made shortbread, so I gave Bill half and put the rest in my lunchbox to eat later.

A Christian Act.

At our very last stop, I opened the van door and heard a loud wailing which seemed to be coming from the bare hawthorn hedge at the side of the road. I got out to investigate and found a thin tortoiseshell cat with two tiny kittens mewing pitifully. *"Oh Bill, look what I've found,"* I called. Bill jumped out of the cab and came to look. He winced when he saw the ragged cat and pathetic kittens huddled under the hedge. *"She must be a stray, or someone's dumped her,"* he commented. At that moment, the old man who owned the cottage where we'd stopped appeared at the door, his library books in his hand. *"What's there?"* he asked, peering under the hedge. I showed him the distressing sight and asked: *"Do you know who they belong to?"* *"No idea, and I don't like cats either. Dogs are my friends, I've two to defend the cottage,"* he said belligerently. *"Oh surely..."* I began weakly. But he was already in the van looking for books. *"Bill, we can't just leave them here to die at Christmas time can we? I've two cats of my own and they wouldn't take kindly to strangers. What are we to do?"* For an answer, Bill rooted in the back of the library van and produced a cardboard box. *"Let's put them in here for now, out of the cold, until we can decide what to do,"* he suggested. *"They can sleep in my garage for tonight and I'll feed the mother, then when you come to work tomorrow we'll see what we can do,"* he added kindly, sensing my distress for the poor animals. And so it was done. The old man chose his books, grumpily wished us a *"Merry Christmas,"* and slammed the door of his cottage. The cat and her kittens seemed settled in the warm box in the bottom of which I'd put newspaper and an old woollen scarf of mine.

Safe out of the freezing wind and rain, the mother cat purred weakly as I tickled her chin on the way back to Ramsbottom. So, I told Penny and Heidi about the cat and her kittens and they were most anxious to find her a home. *"Mummy, please let's keep her,"* pleaded Heidi. *"We've already got two cats, they'd fight"* I assured her. Never the less, I was determined that she and her kittens would find a new, happy home for Christmas.

Market Place, Ramsbottom: the Grant Arms oversees everything.

Next morning I asked Bill how the cat and her kittens were faring. *"Fine,"* said Bill, *"I fed the mother and she was ravenous – mustn't have eaten for days, poor thing,"* he commented. *"Any ideas on a home for her?"* I enquired. *"Well,"* began Bill slowly, *"there's an old man who does the night watch at Brooks' Mill near Summerseat. I saw him last weekend and he'd just lost his cat that kept him company at the mill. Maybe we could ask him if he'd take her and the kittens until they are big enough to be found a home."* *"Oh please let's try. Can we call on him now?"* I pleaded. Bill smiled at me. *"We're passing near his house today, so I'll stop there and we can ask him."* I was full of hope, so we loaded our bags into the van and drove up Bolton Road, Ramsbottom, towards Holcombe Brook and turned left at the 'Hare and Hounds' towards Bury, then left again at Newcombe Road. We made two stops on the estate, then travelled towards Summerseat. Bill stopped the van by a row of little old cottages I'd never noticed before.

He knocked at a nicely painted green door and a wrinkled old face with rosy cheeks appeared. *"This is Joe Ashton,"* said Bill, introducing the old man to me. Bill and I explained about the stray and her kittens and Joe smiled as I asked him breathlessly *"Have you got a new cat yet to keep you company?"* *"Not yet,"* said old Joe and lit his pipe. *"Oh please give Pixie (as I'd secretly christened her because she was so tiny) a good home at the mill. She'll catch mice for you okay, as tortoiseshell cats are the best hunters."* I knew this from experience, as one of my own pets was a tortoiseshell and an excellent hunter, as I regularly found to my dismay gruesome bodies of decapitated shrews on my doorstep. Joe's crinkly cheeks wrinkled even more as he looked at my face. *"How old's the kittens?"* he asked

Bill. *"About three weeks,"* Bill replied. *"Maybe we can find homes for them when they're old enough,"* I suggested. *"Well now, you bring her round to me at the mill tonight,"* old Joe said to Bill, *"and we'll see what she's like."* Much comforted and relieved, I murmured my thanks and we continued our calls in the village of Summerseat, which was quite small in those days, then headed for Affetside.

Over the weekend, I though about Pixie and her kittens, but I needn't have worried, as on the Monday morning, Bill told me that old Joe had quite taken to Pixie and her kittens as well. She would be well looked after and would be company on his night shifts.

Simple Pleasures.

We were to finish our rota on Friday, December 23rd, as Christmas Day was on a Sunday. The Mobile Library would be serviced in the interim period and we would begin our rounds again on January 2nd. This last week was hectic, with pensioners' parties galore, carol services in many of the villages and a wide variety of entertainment in each locality. The villagers relied on their own talents for their Christmas entertainment in those days. At one of the churches in Brinscall, they held a 'Converzatione' (a 'Converzat' for short) which was a kind of church social with many games and dances: I heard all about it in the library van the day after. *"Best yet,"* declared Bertha Parker adjusting her top teeth, *"Ken Thomas looked good as the fairy on top of the Christmas tree,"* chortled another. *"I enjoyed the Velita, but I kept getting mixed up with this thing called 'The Slosh',"* said Edna Turner, a very plump matron of unfathomable age. *"First time we've had a drinks licence,"* commented George Banks dourly. *"It's a wonder the PCC allowed it. I'm surprised at them."*

The Marsh Lane WI had arranged a concert and carol service for the Tuesday night before Christmas. I heard all about it the day after when we visited the village. Elsie Barnes and her sister Doris Booth were two elderly widows not renowned for their jocularity, being known locally as 'the Black Widows' on account of their sombre dress. Yet on this particular occasion, they seemed very jolly and red-faced as they swung into the van with their piles of books, colliding with the other readers who failed to move out of the way quickly enough. I was surprised to smell a faint hint of sherry on their breath and wondered what had happened to the old ladies' morals, until I saw the nods and winks between the other readers in the van. The WI members who'd been in the concert had all been invited to a Christmas lunch the day after and before our library van arrived. The younger members had evidently 'over-indulged' the two straight-laced sisters, as they did every year, and were as amused at the effects of unaccustomed alcohol as I was. There was much stifled giggling as Elsie suddenly burst into 'Deck the halls' and Doris intoned *'Ding dong merrily on high'*. Such merriment from these two old dragons amused everyone for weeks afterwards.

The spire of St.Anne's Church looks down over Turton.

Christmas Card Scenes.

All that last week, at every farm and village, we were offered mince pies, coffee, pork, sherry, shortbread – all kinds of Christmas fayre and my readers were kinder than ever. It was wonderful to travel along the country lanes and to see the pine and spruce trees stretching arms up to the sky to catch the flakes of snow as they whirled down. *"A white Christmas this year,"* said old Mr. Higson. *"Nay!"* responded Tom Haworth. *"We'll be lucky if this lot lies 'til Christmas Day."* We cruised along Bolton Road through Hawkshaw and down towards Bradshaw. On the right was the majesty of Winter Hill looking like a Swiss mountain with a crust of snow on his crown. Dinner was enjoyed at Bromley Cross library, where Mrs. Footitt made us welcome as ever, then over to Egerton. It was a lovely time. In every village, fairy lights twinkled in windows or on tiny Christmas trees. When enough snow had fallen, children sledged on tin trays or in plastic dishes if they hadn't got the real thing. The village shops, bedecked with tinsel and trimmings, did a roaring trade; children wrote notes to Santa Claus and posted them up the chimney, just as I did years ago and as my own two daughters did. As we rushed home through the gathering dusk, our readers' good wishes rang in our ears: *"Merry Christmas, Mrs. Moore. Merry Christmas, Bill. Have a lovely time."*

"What lovely, wonderful people they all are," I thought as I drove home on Decemebr 23rd, my bag full of tokens of love and kindness. They were truly 'Lancashire Natives' of the very best kind.

Epilogue

In 1972, the wind of change began to blow through my idyllic life, in the shape of *'Big Brother'* and Local Government Re-organisation. We were told that from April 1st 1974 my little world of the Mobile Library would cease to exist (literally, that is). Our HQ at Ramsbottom would be disbanded and then belong to Bury; Harwood and Bromley Cross to Bolton; Belmont, Tockholes and parts of Turton to Rossendale for Mobile Library purposes. The precious communities of Abbey Village, Withnell and Brinscall would go to Chorley and so on! I was saddened by all this, but *'All good things come to an end'*, I told myself and, after all, I'd had another few splendid years enjoying my job to the full. The Mobile Library Service was still carrying on, of course, but in fragmented separate areas now.

Later, I began to work part-time in Oswaldtwistle Library where the readers were equally warm and friendly. Looking back over my Mobile Library years, I can safely say they made me even more proud of being ***'Lancashire born and bred, and a true Lancashire Native'***.